MUSIC for HOMESCHOOLERS

A Guide to Music Instruction for the Homeschooled Child

JOANNE MAY

Published by
Meredith Music Publications
a division of G.W. Music, Inc.
4899 Lerch Creek Ct., Galesville, MD 20765
http://www.meredithmusic.com

MEREDITH MUSIC PUBLICATIONS and its stylized double M logo
are trademarks of
MEREDITH MUSIC PUBLICATIONS, a division of G.W. Music, Inc.

Cover and text design: Shawn Girsberger

International Standard Book Number: 978-1-57463-157-9
Cataloging-in-Publication Data is on file with the Library of Congress.
Library of Congress Control Number: 2009938754
Printed and bound in U.S.A

Contents

Acknowledgments... vii

Preface ix

CHAPTER 1
What Does the Research Say About Music Education?..1

Brain Development 1

Age Matters 4

Standardized Test Scores 6

Intelligence Development... 8

Socialization 10

What People Say About Music Education........................ 12

CHAPTER 2
Finding Music Instruction to Fit Your Needs 15

What You Can Do At Home.. 15

*Learn to play an instrument together
with your children*..20

*Get to know a professional musician and ask for
ideas and assistance*..21

*Find materials that will help teach you and
your children to play an instrument*................................21

Sing together often. 22

Encourage your children to listen critically.....................23

Stretch your children just beyond their ability. 24

Have fun with music. *27*

Get your extended family involved. *29*

Record your family's musical activities. *29*

Don't be apologetic if you lack
formal musical training *30*

Be your children's greatest cheerleader. *30*

Private Instruction Options 31

Community Programs *31*

Youth Symphonies *33*

Music Schools *33*

Summer Camps *36*

Homeschool Groups *37*

College and University Programs *38*

Competitions *39*

Adult Instruction *40*

Public Music Options 40

Local Library Programs *40*

Park District and Community College Offerings *40*

Public School Music Programs *41*

CHAPTER 3

Organizations That Offer Support 45

Standards Publications: The Arts 46

Standards Publications: Music 46

MENC Position Paper 47

Homeschooled Students' Participation in Public School
Music Education *47*

Support Organizations for Music Education 52

Additional Organizations 62

CHAPTER 4
Advice From Homeschool Families

Advice From Homeschool Families.............................. 65

Family #1 66
Family #2 69
Family #3 71
Family #4 74
Family #5 76
Family #6 78
Family #7 79

CHAPTER 5
Some Issues For Consideration

Some Issues For Consideration................................82

Eligibility/Fit of the Program 83
Recruitment of Homeschoolers Into the School Program....85
Instrument Rental or Purchase 87
Individual and Group Lessons................................ 90
Finding a Private Teacher 92
Commitment to Systematic Learning....................... 94
Practicing.. 96
Technology 98
College Admissions 99
Parents and Teachers as Role Models 102

CHAPTER 6
Additional Resources

Additional Resources..107

Publishers and Printed Music 107
Software and Music Technology 109
Websites... 113
Conclusion.. 118

Endnotes...119
About the Author...121

Acknowledgments

||||||||||||||||||||||||||||||||||||||||||||||||||||||||||||||||||||||||||||||||

To Garwood Whaley, President and Founder of Meredith Music Publications, I offer my deepest gratitude and thanks for having the insight to realize the need for this book, and for inviting me to write it. Gar is constantly challenging himself to find areas of need in the music education literature, and he has single handedly made a *huge* impact on music educators and all those who benefit from music instruction through the works published by his company. Not only is he an outstanding musician and educator of the highest order, but he is also a successful entrepreneur with courage, passion and commitment to excellence. I owe him my greatest debt of gratitude for this wonderful opportunity.

My sincere thanks to the many homeschool families who graciously offered of their time, talents, and expertise for the chapter on "Advice From Homeschool Families." They are the true experts – parents who have taken on the risks and responsibilities of homeschooling, made choices for their children's musical education, and who have successful stories to tell. The details of their journeys are all unique and different, and it became obvious through our conversations that they have a clear vision of the goals for their children, a deep commitment to educating their children in music, and an open willingness to share what they've learned with others who are seeking advice. They are the true heroes and heroines in this educational arena.

Finally, thanks to the thousands of homeschool families in this country who have made learning music a priority in their lives, and to their music instructors who every day not only teach, but inspire students, nurturing them in the lifelong development of musicianship and character.

Preface

|||||||||||||||||||||||||||||||||||||||||||||||||||||||||||||||||||||||||||||||||||||||||

When I began researching the field for literature on homeschool music instruction, I found very little published information to help guide families in the musical education of their
children. With the rising numbers of homeschoolers in the United
States and numerous research studies that prove the powerful
impact of music instruction on a child's social and intellectual
development, it became apparent that a book to assist parents
in musical pursuits for their children, and teachers who are interested in learning more about homeschoolers and their needs,
would be a valuable addition to the music-education literature.

Garwood Whaley, Founder and President of Meredith Music
Publications, recently came across an article published in the
Washington Post newspaper[1] written by the father of homeschooled children stating that 1) there is a misconception that
homeschooling was started and is being maintained by "religious fanatics" when in fact today's homeschoolers come from
a wide variety of backgrounds; 2) homeschoolers are changing
the face of education in our country as a result of the tremen-
dous growth in this movement; and 3) parents benefit when
they homeschool their children because they have the freedom
to make educational choices that they believe are good for their

children and are not plugged into a pre-determined curriculum that may include elements they find objectionable.

The U.S. Department of Education National Center for Education Statistics (NCES) published reports in 1999[2], 2003[3], and 2007[4] showing the growth in the U.S. homeschool population. Data estimates are based on parent surveys from the National Household Education Surveys Program (NHES) of children ages five to seventeen. In 1999 there were approximately 850,000 children homeschooled in America, in 2003 there were approximately 1,096,000, and in 2007 there were approximately 1,508,000. This is an increase of 658,000 students, almost doubling the population of homeschoolers in our country in just eight years. Reasons cited why parents are choosing to homeschool, in order of greatest to least significant importance, are concerns about the school environment, a desire to provide religious and moral instruction, a dissatisfaction with academic instruction in schools, wanting a nontraditional approach to their child's education, having a child with special needs, and having a child with a physical or mental health problem.

Parents of homeschoolers want the best education possible for their children, and are willing to take responsibility to teach them and to find creative ways to offer meaningful and exciting learning experiences for them. Repeatedly in my interviews with them, parents talked about the importance of the freedom to choose their children's curriculum. They want to teach them moral and ethical values, offer them religious instruction as a part of their daily routine, and have the flexibility to design a schedule that maximizes time-of-day issues their children face.

Young children who focus best in the morning and teenagers who peak in their ability to concentrate in the afternoon or evening can reap the benefit of a schedule designed to accommodate these differences in the homeschool family. Having the flexibility to go hear a world-class musician during school hours, or the freedom to get together for music making with other homeschool families during the daytime, is of high value to homeschool parents who have the option of going on a "field trip" on any given day for these purposes. Having the freedom to design individualized activities for each of their children gives parents more control over the learning experiences and accomplishments of their children. If parents are able to decide on a curriculum and schedule for their children that reflects their own values, for example to teach creationism instead of evolution, or to schedule practicing a musical instrument in the first part of the day instead of following a traditional school schedule that usually leaves practicing to the end of the child's day, then the children's learning, interests, abilities and skills can be maximized according to the priorities parents set for their children.

The parent who is most effective as a homeschool "teacher" is one who becomes very savvy about seeking out others who can offer instruction and experiences in areas in which they are not experts. Parents who homeschool their children do not necessarily possess the tools or skills needed to teach their children everything they will need to know throughout their school-age years. Groups of families often coordinate their efforts by having their children travel from home to home while the parents teach a single subject or a particular age of children. Homeschool support groups have popped up all over the country as families assist other families in the educational process.

Even if a parent has the skills to teach a certain subject or content area, however, it may be in the child's best interest for them to seek the expertise of others, for several reasons. First, the child may learn better when being taught by someone other than the parent because of the difference in personality, timing, and mode of delivery. The child may be willing to strive to attain a higher level of accomplishment with a teacher whom they admire, rather than with the parent. Second, children are very sociable and positively respond to others when they are in group settings of various sizes. The family group can be one of those learning environments, but other larger groups, or groups in which several children are the same age, can offer new and exciting learning modalities for the children. A third reason to seek instruction outside the family is to give the children the opportunity for unique experiences. Students who learn to play an instrument or sing will be enriched when they share their musical accomplishments with others in a concert or recital, especially one that is organized by a teacher that includes other students. Taking a trip with an orchestra, choir, or band to perform in a European cathedral, for example, can have a much deeper musical and emotional impact than the experience of performing in a local mall or church with other members of the family. Participating with other musicians in a symphony performance, playing in a summer outdoor concert, or marching with a band in a parade can offer encouragement and inspiration to children that can't be duplicated without these unique and valuable experiences.

Music instruction can be a mystery to parents who have not had musical training. Parents who consider themselves musicians, and teachers in various stages of their careers, may be looking for ideas to increase their knowledge of how to teach music creatively and effectively to children. It is my hope that this book will serve as a valuable resource to people who hold music education high in their set of values and who, no matter where they live or what background they have in music, will be able to go forth with confidence in selecting and designing high quality musical experiences for children. The ultimate goal is for homeschool parents to become participants with their children as together they learn to develop the skills to love music, and consequently have richer, more enjoyable and meaningful lives.

1

What Does the Research Say About Music Education?

||||||||||||||||||||||||||||||||||||||||||||||||||||||||||||||||||||||||||||||

Brain Development

"Young children who take music lessons show different brain development and improved memory over
the course of a year, compared to children who do not
receive musical training. The brains of musically trained
children respond to music in a different way to those of
untrained children, and the musical training improves
their memory. After one year the musically trained
children performed better in a memory test that is correlated with general intelligence skills such as literacy,
verbal memory, visio spatial processing, mathematics
and IQ." — *Dr. Laurel Trainor, Prof. of Psychology, Neuro-*
science, and Behaviour at McMaster University, Director
of the McMaster Institute for Music and the Mind; Can-
ada; published 9/20/06; <http://www.sciencedaily.com/
releases/2006/09/060920093024.htm>

Lydia (whose name has been changed to protect her identity) lives in a suburb of Chicago and didn't speak until she was four years old. The doctors said she had a neurological disorder, but misdiagnosed its type and prescribed improper medications to treat her. While her family struggled to find the right balance of physical, social, and intellectual activities to inspire her and to help her learn and develop, they also did what proved to be the most valuable asset to her development—they listened to her when she indicated a desire to learn to play the cello.

Lydia's mother is an amateur pianist, who found playing piano an enjoyable outlet to the stresses of life. Daily she would sit down at the piano to play and sing. When Lydia was a very young child, she would sit with her back pressed up against the soundboard of the piano so her whole body could feel the vibrations of the music. She had a look of great happiness on her face while her mother played, and the music had a wonderfully calming effect on her. Then one day, at the age of four, Lydia brought a picture to her mother, and, having learned to speak only in sign language, gestured that she wanted to play the instrument in the photograph. The picture was of a cello Lydia had found in a magazine.

Lydia's parents discussed lessons for her, but were skeptical that without her ability to speak, she would have great difficulty learning and responding appropriately to a teacher. However, the doctors encouraged her parents by saying that group experiences would be good for her social and verbal development, so they began calling their friends and talking to "musical" people they knew to find a music instructor. In their suburban area there were many options, and they narrowed them down by explaining their needs to the teachers they had found: they were looking for group lessons, experiences that didn't require reading, and above all, flexibility, since Lydia's development was not progressing at a normal pace. They were fortunate to find an exact fit in a local Suzuki cello program, and there they found great success.

Lydia's teacher took her passion for the cello and molded it, challenging her in areas where she could handle the challenge, and making adjustments specifically for her in areas where she needed to take a path somewhat different than the average cello student. With much hard work, patience, consistent practice and nurturing, Lydia has become an outstanding musician. Today she is thriving in a public high school, succeeding in all academic classes and excelling as an accomplished member of the cello section of the school's symphony orchestra. According to the research, without her early music instruction Lydia's academic, verbal, and social progress would have developed at a slower pace and at a lower level. Through her musical training Lydia's memory improved, positively affecting her general intelligence, especially in her weakest areas of verbal language and literacy skills.

Here's another research finding connecting the mastering of a musical instrument and language development:

"A 2004 Stanford University study showed that mastering a musical instrument improves the way the human brain processes parts of spoken language. In two studies, researchers demonstrated that people with musical experience found it easier than non-musicians to detect small differences in word syllables. They also discovered that musical training helps the brain work more efficiently in distinguishing split-second differences between rapidly changing sounds that are essential to processing language. About 40 adults, divided into groups of musicians and non-musician, matched by age, sex, general language ability and intelligence, were tested. To qualify, the musicians need to have started playing instruments before age 7 and never stopped, practicing several hours/week. Functional magnetic resonance imaging showed the musicians had more focused, efficient brain activity. This is the first example showing how musical training alters how your brain processes language components." — *Prof. John Gabrieli, former Stanford psychology professor, now associate director of MIT's Athinoula A. Martinos Center for Biomedical Imaging.<http://news-service.stanford.edu>, Nov. 2005)*

Age Matters

"A study of 31 children found that children who received keyboard instruction for two years beginning at age 3 continued to score higher on spatial-temporal and arithmetic tasks two years after the instruction was terminated (Rauscher & LeMieux, 2003). The age at which children begin instruction appears to affect the duration of extra-musical cognitive outcomes, and longitudinal research suggests that at least two years of music instruction are required for sustained enhancement of spatial abilities." (Rauscher, 2002); *ERIC Clearinghouse on Early Education and Parenting, Can Music Instruction Affect Children's Cognitive Development? ERIC Digest; Frances H. Rauscher; ERIC Identifier: ED480540, Publication Date: 09/2003. <http://www.ericdigests.org/2004-3/cognitive.html>*

Suzuki lessons, Kindermusik, Yamaha Piano lessons and many other early childhood music programs offer instruction in instrumental and vocal music to children as young as three years of age. There are programs all across the country that have had much success for a variety of reasons: parents become directly involved in their children's education developing a rapport and commonality with their children as life-long learners; children's interactions with the teacher, parent and other children allow them the opportunity to develop skills such as cooperation and respect they may not necessarily develop in academic pursuits; music is intrinsically motivating and children are naturally attracted to want to learn; the discipline of learning new concepts/skills and then practicing them repeatedly teaches children how to have discipline and success in many other areas; these programs begin very early — I've witnessed children as young as eighteen months of age participating in Suzuki violin lessons — and many parents have experienced such good outcomes with their children that their witness to others has become the perpetuating strength of these programs.

Music lessons give children the brain structures to learn systematically, learning to master concepts and skills before moving to the next higher level. Shinichi Suzuki calls this the "mother tongue approach" to learning — just as a parent encourages a baby to first babble, then form syllables, words, and sentences while consistently repeating all that has previously been learned. This teaches children perseverance, success at reasoning and problem solving skills, and the ability to organize thought. As the research has proven, spatial-temporal and arithmetic tasks show higher scores in children who have studied music, continuing to positively affect the brain even after music instruction has ended.

Further, in this study by Nina Kraus:

> "Playing a musical instrument significantly enhances the brainstem's sensitivity to speech sounds. This relates to

encoding skills involved with music and language. Experience with music at a young age can "fine-tune" the
brain's auditory system." — *from a study supported by
Northwestern University, grants from the National Insti-
tutes of Health, and the National Science Foundation. Nina
Kraus, director of NWU's Auditory Neuroscience Labora-
tory and senior author of the study, which appeared in April
2007 Nature Neuroscience. Other contributing researchers/
authors: Patrick Wong, primary author "Musical Experience
Shapes Human Brainstem Encoding of Linguistic Pitch Patterns." Other researchers Erika Skoe, Nicole Russo, Tasha
Dees; info from <www.sciencedaily.com>*

Standardized Test Scores

Schools are in an ongoing battle to improve standardized test
scores, both as a result of No Child Left Behind and in their
efforts to report good results to the stakeholders in their districts and communities. Homeschoolers, as well, are looking
toward the future when their children will be required to take
standardized tests for college entrance and beyond. Both the
College Board and the Journal of Research in Music Education
have reported recent findings on the study of music and how it
relates to standardized test outcomes:

The College Board

"Students of the arts continue to outperform their non-
arts peers on the SAT, according to reports by the College
Entrance Examination Board. In 2006, SAT takers with
coursework/experience in music performance scored 57
points higher on the verbal portion of the test and 43
points higher on the math portion than students with

no coursework or experience in the arts. Scores for those with coursework in music appreciation were 62 points higher on the verbal and 41 points higher on the math portion." — *The Student Descriptive Questionnaire, a self-reported component of the SAT that gathers information about students' academic preparation, gathered data for these reports. Source: The College Board, Profile of College-Bound Seniors National Report for 2006; <http://www.collegeboard.com>*

MENC Journal of Research in Music Education

"Students in high-quality school music programs score higher on standardized tests compared to students in schools with deficient music education programs, regardless of the socioeconomic level of the school or school district. Students in top-quality music programs scored 22% better in English and 20% better in math than students in deficient music programs. Students in top-quality instrumental programs scored 19% higher in English than students in schools without a music program. Students in top quality instrumental programs scored 17% higher in math than children in schools without a music program. Students at schools with excellent music programs had higher English and math test scores across the country than students in schools with low-quality music programs. Students in all regions with lower-quality instrumental programs scored higher in English and math than students who had no music at all." — *MENC Journal of Research in Music Education, Winter 2006, vol. 54, No. 4, pgs. 293- 307; "Examination of Relationship between Participation in School Music Programs of Differing*

Quality and Standardized Test Results," Christopher M. Johnson and Jenny E. Memmott, University of Kansas.

Intelligence Development

Intelligence, once thought to be immutable, or unchangeable, can be improved according to a recent study. By giving the brain challenging activities, a person's ability to more quickly, clearly, and accurately process information has led researchers to conclude that one's intelligence can be altered over time. In a study published in April, 2008 entitled "Improving fluid intelligence with training on working memory," co-author and post-doctorate fellow at the University of Michigan Susanne M. Jaeggi states that:

"Intelligence has always been considered principally an immutable inherited trait. Our results show you can increase your intelligence with appropriate training." — National Academy of Sciences, Department of Psychology, University of Michigan, Department of Psychology, University of Bern, co-authors Susanne M. Jaeggi, Martin Buschkuehl, John Jonides, Walter J. Perrig, edited by Edward E. Smith, Columbia University, New York, NY, and approved March 18, 2008 (received for review February 7, 2008).

The activities that improve fluid intelligence include doing two tasks at the same time, monitoring performance of the tasks, sorting relevant and irrelevant information, and connecting similar or related items. While this study does not specifically measure the performance of musical activities, the requirements of playing a musical instrument or singing are immediately apparent when considering this list of activities. The instrumental music student is required to perform different functions in both hands simultaneously, and all musicians must make judgments about the quality of the music being played, prioritize the focus of certain skills over others, and understand the connection of one type of performance technique to another.

Following is a study comparing IQ data of students who had music lessons with those who had no lessons or who studied drama:

"Results of an IQ test given to groups of children (total: 144) who were provided with lessons in keyboard, voice, drama or no lessons at all, showed that the IQ of students in the keyboard or voice classes increased from their pre-lesson IQ score, more than the IQ of those students taking drama or no lessons. Generally these increases occurred across IQ subtests, index scores, and academic achievement." — *Summary by MENC; Original source: August 2004, Psychological Science, a journal of the American Psychological Society; <http://www.psychologicalscience.org/pdf/ps/musiciq.pdf>; Dr. E. Glenn Schellenberg (University of Toronto).*

Verbal memory is also positively affected in children with musical training:

"Children with music training had significantly better verbal memory than those without such training, and the longer the training, the better the verbal memory. Researchers studied 90 boys between the ages of 6 and 15. Half had musical training as members of their school's string orchestra program, plus lessons in playing classical music on Western instruments like the flute or violin for one to five years. The other 45 students had no training. Students with musical training recalled more words in a verbal memory test than did untrained students, and after a 30-minute delay, students with training also retained more words than the control group. In a follow-up one year later, students who continued training and beginners who had just started learning to play both showed improvement in verbal learning and retention." — *Summary by MENC. Original source: Ho, Y. C., Cheung, M. C., & Chan, A. Music training improves verbal but not visual memory: cross-sectional and longitudinal explorations in children (2003) Neuropsychology, 12, 439-450.*

Socialization

A comprehensive program of musical activities includes a combination of both individual and group experiences. In the best programs the student learns in individual or group lessons from a teacher, practices independently to perfect the skills learned, then uses the skills in a performance setting with other musicians. Groups can be any size — from two people to hundreds of people — and the exhilaration that comes from performing with others is unparalleled in any other part of life.

The social aspect of music making is a much-needed element in today's society. People are working more from their homes, and kids are watching more television and playing more video games than ever before. Group musical activities provide communication between people in a meaningful way, and provide children with the opportunities to develop socialization skills.

"The fact that choral singing is a communal activity is especially significant today when we increasingly rely on internet-based communications, rather than face-to-face interaction. Several recent studies have shown a significant decline in civic engagement in our communities. Robert Putnam, Harvard University's Kennedy School of Government scholar, asserts that the significance of choral singing goes beyond music making, and even beyond the arts. He sees group performing as contributing directly to the social trust and reciprocity that is the basis of civic engagement. His work shows that the mere existence of choral groups helps foster America's democratic culture... Chorus America found that choral singers are far more likely to be involved in charity work, as volunteers and as donors (76 %), than the average person (44% according to a 2001 report by Independent Sector). Choral singers are also more than twice as likely as non-participants to be aware of current events and involved in the political process. They are also twice as likely as the general public to be major consumers of other arts — and not just music." — *America's Performing Art: A Study of Choruses, Choral Singers, and their Impact (Chorus Impact Study, 2003); <www.chorusamerica.org>*

"Secondary students who participated in band or orchestra reported the lowest lifetime and current use of all substances (alcohol, tobacco, illicit drugs)." — *Texas Commission on Drug and Alcohol Abuse Report. Reported in Houston Chronicle, January 1998.*

"Data show that high earnings are not just associated with people who have high technical skills. In fact, mastery of the arts and humanities is just as closely correlated with high earnings, and, according to our analysis, that will continue to be true. History, music, drawing and painting, and economics will give our students an edge just as surely as math and science will." — *Tough Choices or Tough Times: The report of the new commission on the skills of the American workforce, 2007, page 29; <www.skillscommission.org>*

What People Say About Music Education

Many of the parents I talked to had anecdotal stories about how the study of music has made their children smarter, happier, better problem solvers, more confident, more sensitive, and better able to get along with others. The research bears out this anecdotal evidence, and gives support to the position that learning music should be an integral part of every child's curriculum.

Here's what others have said about the study of the arts:

"The life of the arts, far from being an interruption, a distraction, in the life of the nation, is close to the center of a nation's purpose—and is a test to the quality of a nation's civilization." — *John F. Kennedy*

"I have made a career doing things that weren't even invented when I graduated from high school 40 years ago. It will be the same for today's graduates, only on a sharply accelerating timeline. Much of what I learned in the classroom is obsolete or, at best, only marginally useful. What has made a difference in my life has been the ability to learn as I go, to adapt to new ideas, to have the courage to take risks, and to feel confident I will be able to perform and successfully meet the challenges of new situations. These skills I learned through participation in band and drama." — *Fred Behning retired from IBM Corporation after a 32-year career that included assignments in systems engineering, product development, management, and customer technology briefings, and is still an IBM consultant. A life-long musician, Fred plays oboe and English horn in the Williamson County Symphony Orchestra and the Austin Symphonic Band. <http://www.supportmusic.com/ drjohn/archive/2007-06-11.mhtml>*

"Music has a great power for bringing people together. With so many forces in this world acting to drive wedges between people, it's important to preserve those things that help us experience our common humanity." — *Ted Turner, Turner Broadcasting System.*

"Casals says music fills him with the wonder of life and the 'incredible marvel' of being a human. Ives says it expands his mind and challenges him to be a true individual. Bernstein says it is enriching and ennobling. To me, that sounds like a good cause for making music and the arts an integral part of every child's education. Studying music and the arts elevates children's education, expands students' horizons, and teaches them to appreciate the wonder of life." — *U.S. Secretary of Education Richard W. Riley, July 1999.*

"Music is one way for young people to connect with themselves, but it is also a bridge for connecting with others. Through music, we can introduce children to the richness and diversity of the human family and to the myriad rhythms of life." — *Daniel A. Carp, Eastman Kodak Company Chairman and CEO.*

"I dream of a day when every child in America will have in his or her hand a musical instrument, be it a clarinet, a drumstick or a guitar. And I dream of a day when there's no state legislature that would even consider cutting funding for music and the arts because they realize that it's a life skill that changes the lives of students and gives them not only better academic capability, but it makes them better people. We sometimes forget that many of us in this room, including this guy standing right in front of you, would not be where he is today if not for having music introduced in my life because it gave me the understanding of teamwork, discipline and focus." *Mike Huckabee, Former Arkansas Governor; NAMM University Breakfast Sessions 2007, NAMM Playback Magazine, Spring 2007, pg. 36; <www.namm.com>*

_2_

Finding Music Instruction to Fit Your Needs

N ow that you've read the research, let's delve into the exciting possibilities for the musical future of you and your children. The following four types of instruction available to your children will be addressed:

- The instruction you provide for your children

- The instruction you can find in private organizations in your area

- The instruction you can find in public organizations in your area

- Technology for self-instruction (also see Chapter 6)

What You Can Do At Home

Whether you are a professional musician, or one who simply has a passion for music and has never had any formal training, there are many things you can do to encourage your children's love of and skill in music.

From before your child's birth, music can be integrated into your daily routine. Children's minds are natural sponges, especially in the earliest stages of development, and your baby's mind will soak up a variety of sounds if you simply play recordings of high quality and interesting music. Play what you like, but also look for various styles of music to stimulate your baby's mind. The more variety the better!

As a young pregnant teacher, I played recordings of music to classes of my students repetitively. Several weeks before my daughter was born, I experienced many nights of significant fetal activity that kept me awake or woke me from deep slumber. After some frustration with my lack of sleep, I decided to try playing a recording of one of the pieces of music I'd been teaching my students to see if my unborn baby would respond to it. The moment I put on this particular recording, she immediately stopped moving and kicking. The first time this happened I was sure, in my sleepless stupor, I was just imagining her calming down. But night after night, week after week the same thing occurred. Her response was always to immediately slow or stop all activity when I played the music. I became convinced that she recognized the music, even before she was born (see   <http://www.menc.org/resources/view/from-heartbeat-to-steady-beat-music-and-the-unborn-child> for a summary of several important technical medical studies on the effect of music on the unborn).

Creating a musical environment in your home and in your daily life will have an astounding, lasting affect on your children. When children hear the same music repeatedly, they naturally begin to hum, sing, and dance to it. Have you ever watched a very young child run to a television set or radio, dancing and singing the words to an advertisement that has been played many times in the home? Marketers know the astounding and powerful effect of "jingles" that are catchy and repetitive. You can utilize this effective tool to teach music to your children by simply playing recordings of music in your home over and over. Choose classics, children's songs, jazz, country, blue grass, rock, big band, Christian praise music, pop, vocal, instrumental, and music of various cultures — the more different types you play the better. As they listen, your children will hear the variations in tempo, range, dynamics, and expressive qualities of the music. Move to the music together with your child, and try to imitate what you're hearing through your movements. This activity will provide an excellent non-verbal form of expression for your child, and will aid you in understanding what your child is hearing in the music.

When Shinichi Suzuki designed his method to teach the children of Japan how to play violin, he required the parents and children to listen many times every day to the music the child would soon be learning to play. He understood the importance of listening in the musical development of the child, and expected families to listen to professional recordings in their homes daily, starting before birth if possible. His philosophy is that every child can learn, and children will learn best the same way they learn to speak and understand a complex language — he calls it the "mother-tongue approach." Children should listen both passively and actively, just as they do when they are learning to speak. To listen passively, simply put on a recording of a piece of music and let it play while the family does other activities such as riding in a car, doing household chores, or getting ready for bed. For active listening, give full attention to the music, sitting quietly while following the musical score and taking note of the structure, form, dynamics, rhythmic patterns, etc., and then discussing these musical elements. Active listening allows children to consciously process and analyze the music, and gives them the opportunity to reflect on their observations.

For active listening, choose a piece of music to listen to with your children, and after a portion of the piece is played, stop the recording and discuss what you've just heard. Did the music go up or go down? Make gestures to indicate the flow and direction. Was it loud or soft? Show loudness with large gestures and softness with small ones. At a more advanced level, what instruments or voices did you hear? Was there anything that repeated? Were the repeats exact or were they slightly different each time? How many performers do you think there were? Was there a melody? Was it a male or female voice singing the melody? What instrument kept the beat? Try to discover different things in the music with each listening.

In active listening, you also can have your children draw pictures of what they're listening to, or act out what they hear in the music. After multiple times listening to the piece, ask your children to outline the structure of the music. Keep it simple and use language your children can understand. Were there only two large sections of music, each different (A-B form, or you can call it "salt and pepper" form)? Did you hear a repeat of the first section at the end (A-B-A form, or "sandwich" form)? What about the rhythmic and dynamic effect of the music? Did it sound loud, fast, and driving? Soft, smooth, and quiet? What rhythmic patterns did you hear? Can you tap the patterns on your leg? Have your children use analogies for the music (eg: "this sounds like 100 elephants trampling a corn field", or "that sounds like cars racing along a highway in Iceland"). Have fun, and don't be afraid to be silly. Let your ears guide you, and you may discover that you'll hear things in the music you've never heard before. Even if you don't know the musical terms to use when you're listening with your children, you will be stimulating their creativity and enjoyment of the music, while encouraging critical listening skills. Learning the vocabulary can come after the listening, as an outgrowth of the process.

Be cautious about two things when you're listening to music: don't choose music that is so loud that it might damage your child's hearing, and don't play the same piece or style of music exclusively. Our brains are programmed for variety, and learning is greater when we are stimulated by various sounds and styles.

Let's say you've accomplished many listening activities with your children and they are excited about music. They love to sing along with their favorite songs, and they're beginning to have an appreciation and understanding of a variety of styles of music. Now you're ready to take them to a higher level. You may know that they don't always sing in tune or in time and you want to encourage them to improve these skills. You can hear that they're not always with the beat and you'd like to be able to teach them accurate rhythmic skills. Maybe you don't know whether they have any "talent" or whether you could take them any further in their musical training. What next?

Remember the research study on fluid intelligence. Your child's intelligence can improve over time given appropriate challenging activities and training. Teaching your child to identify similarities and differences, to do two tasks at the same time, and to sort out what is relevant and what is not will ensure a rigorous and successful journey toward musical accomplishment. You will aid in the process by monitoring how well these tasks are being done, and making regular adjustments in the immediate goals to be sure they continue to be appropriate and reasonable. Children who work diligently and steadily at activities that are challenging just beyond their reach will not be frustrated that the concepts and skills are either too easy or too difficult. Teachers can attest to having students they never thought would be able to learn, suddenly seem to have amazing success. Their success is not really sudden, but the result of steady progress taken in small steps that result in a culminating accomplishment. Once you make the commitment that teaching your children the gift of music is worth your efforts, you *will* be successful, just as all children who learn to speak in their native tongue are successful at learning a language that is foreign to them. The key to success is the commitment to steady progress taken at a pace that is appropriate for the child.

Here is a list of experiences you can provide for your children to take them on the journey to their next level of musicianship:

Learn to play an instrument together with your children.

Find an instrument that makes sense to you and your family. If you have a guitar or an accordion in the attic, get it down, take it to a local instrument repair shop and have it refurbished. If you already know how to play or just need a refresher, find your old method book, dust it off, and start practicing! Your children will be intrigued and will want to play, too. Schedule about thirty minutes a week for each child to have a lesson with you, and set a daily practice schedule for them. Teach them the basics, just the way you learned them. You may need to anticipate the problems your children will have before starting to teach them. Are their arms and fingers long enough to reach the notes on the instrument? Will they want to perform a whole song the first time they pick up the instrument, and get frustrated when they can't? What if they haven't learned to read music and can't read your method book? Can you show them ways to overcome these problems?

Make a practice plan for them to follow during their daily routine, and be specific about how many repetitions they should do for each activity. They'll be much more likely to want to do the practicing if you offer them structure and set expectations. Their reward will come when they finally accomplish playing a piece of music. You should stay at least one or two lessons ahead of your children in your own performance skills, and while you practice on your own keep in mind what their needs might be. Consider their ages, stages of development, and abilities, and keep a notebook of your ideas by writing lesson plans for them.

Get to know a professional musician and ask for ideas and assistance.

Your church choir director, neighborhood piano teacher, middle school band director, or musician friends can be great resources for you when you have musical questions. Tell them you are homeschooling your children and that you're trying to encourage them daily to love music and to develop musical skills. Ask them specific questions such as, "How do you teach a child to sing on pitch? What instruments would NOT be good choices for my children given their stature and size? At what age did you start formal musical training with your children? What method books, literature, and music technology do you recommend? Who should I go to for assistance in purchasing an instrument?" etc. Professional musicians are very giving people, and you may develop some lifelong friendships!

Find materials that will help teach you and your children to play an instrument.

"Play Today — A Complete Guide to the Basics" for guitar, bass guitar, drums, piano, alto saxophone, flute, clarinet, trumpet, and violin is published by the Hal Leonard Corporation. The series is advertised as "the ultimate self-teaching series" and includes basic information on posture, technique, tone production, and note reading, as well as a professional-quality CD with full-demo tracks and audio instruction. The books are written by expert authors. Many other materials, including books, CDs, DVDs, and music educational software, are available by various publishers for self-teaching and for individual lessons. Be sure to look for method books that contain basic playing information, as well as recordings or DVD's for you to listen to or watch. More information on available materials can be found in Chapter 6.

Sing together often.

Singing as a family regularly from an early age makes a huge impact on your child's musical development. Children naturally love to sing as they develop their ability to speak a language, even as infants. When you provide ideas for your children by singing songs all day long, your children will gradually develop the ability to imitate your songs. Find recordings of developmentally appropriate children's songs to learn and sing along with them at various times throughout the day—in the car when you're driving somewhere, while having a snack, during chore time, etc. Children's concert videos are available (our favorites were *Raffi* and *Rosenshantz*), and these offer children opportunities to participate in the songs with a leader guiding them on how and what to sing. Also, you can learn and teach your children "call and response" songs, in which you sing a phrase and your children respond with another phrase. When your children sing their responses, you have the opportunity to hear their voices more clearly than if you are singing along with them, giving you a better idea how accurately they're matching pitch and singing in rhythm.

When my children were very young, we sang our way through the day, making up creative words to familiar melodies and creating new tunes about the most mundane tasks. I also set aside some time every evening, as they were getting ready for bed, to read a story and then sing songs. They couldn't go to bed without the songs — it just became part of our routine. My daughter always asked for more songs, and I would rack my brain to sing every song I'd ever learned and could remember. My son was usually grumpy and when he'd heard me sing enough he would say, "stop singing mommy!" Some years later I asked him if he remembered telling me as a toddler to stop singing, and why he'd said that to me. His response was, "I remember that I had other music in my head and your singing was interfering with it!" Today both of my children cannot imagine living their lives without music — it has become a part of their identity.

As children become ready for more musical challenges, encourage them to take leadership roles to teach others or lead a family song, sing harmony on the last note of a song or throughout a song, create a complimentary rhythmic pattern by tapping on their legs or vocalizing syllables, or improvise words during a portion of a verse. The possibilities are endless!

Encourage your children to listen critically.

When you actively listen to recordings with your children, promote high-order thinking. Open ended questions such as, "what do you think the music is going to do next?" and "why do you think the composer chose to make this music so long?" begin to encourage your children's creativity, and prompts other questions in their minds that may need to be answered first. For example, they may need to know the historical context for the music, they may need to know other works by the composer and how this piece relates to those works, or they may need to understand common patterns of music in the same genre in order to know whether this piece follows the normal patterns or breaks tradition.

While you and your children are participating in musical activities — singing, playing, or moving to music — ask them to analyze specific elements in the music. For example, "When you're marching to this music, what instrument do you hear every time your foot hits the floor? What do you hear when your foot is lifted? When you and your brother are singing the last note of your favorite song, can you make your voices match up so well that you actually sound like only one person singing? Can you name two instruments that are playing in this section of the music?" If you are confident in knowing music well enough to hear your children make improvements in their performance after they listen critically to their music, celebrate with them! If your ear is not telling you whether they've made adjustments accurately, don't worry. Simply by asking them to listen encourages a higher level of musical development. That is grounds for celebration as well!

Stretch your children just beyond their ability.

Based on brain research, in order for children to have success in learning educators suggest that they should do activities and learn skills that are just out of their reach. A level too low would be boring, and a level too high would be frustrating. You are the monitor of what is appropriate for your children, and you will need to constantly gauge where they stand in the learning continuum given their prior knowledge and experience. Don't assume that if you have one child who learns in a certain way or at a certain pace, your other children will do the same. Each child learns in a unique way (to view a chart of brain-based teaching strategies see *Caine, R.N., Caine, G. October, 1990. Understanding a Brain Based Approach to Learning and Teaching. Educational Leadership 48, 2, 66-70. <http://www.sedl.org/sci-math/compass/v03n02/1.html>)*

As an example, when teaching your children how to play an instrument, begin by demonstrating what you want them to do, then ask them to try it. This is, in effect, a "pre-test" for knowledge and skill. When I teach violin vibrato I know there are many steps to learning this skill, but occasionally a student can just do vibrato without much instruction. There's no need to put this student through the rigors of "waving, tapping, brushing, sticking thumb, changing position, sticking finger, repeat!" if the student is already coordinated and relaxed enough to do vibrato at first attempt. If, on the other hand, the first attempt produces great tension, very little coordination of movement, and little understanding of the goal of vibrato, it will be necessary to teach the student how to practice exercises that build the skills required to do vibrato. For this student, I design exercises in incremental steps that the student is capable of performing, but that need repetition for fluency and speed, building from one skill to another until the whole vibrato motion is learned.

Find out what your children can already do or what they know before determining where to begin. You may be surprised at how much your children have learned from each other, from sources outside the home, or what innate natural abilities they may have. Some children will be able to sing on pitch without much assistance, and others will need a great deal of help making their voices go high and low before landing on a particular note. Adjust your lessons according to their readiness for a skill or concept. If, for example, your child is slow to develop fine motor control, give him exercises in finger dexterity so he will develop confidence and fluency. Be sure to choose exercises that are appropriate for the lesson and for his level — for example, ones that he can do slowly but needs to do repetitively in order to gain speed. As he begins to gain dexterity, he will develop confidence, and with that confidence he will soon be ready to move to the next level or skill. You will see his enthusiasm for learning when you've chosen appropriate activities.

Method books, written by expert authors and teachers who have students' various learning styles in mind, are available to assist you in determining effective lesson plans for your children (see Chapter 6 for some current publications). However, if you come upon a page or unit of concepts your child already knows, take the initiative to move forward, or go back to review previously learned material. Keep the "mother-tongue" approach always in mind — as your children learn new skills, continue to review old ones. Keep them from boredom by challenging them to perform their old skills at a new level. For example, in the Suzuki Violin School there are ten books or levels — when book three-level students practice songs in book one, they should sound like book three students, not book one students. The differences are subtle, but should be noticeable in every aspect of the music — tone, rhythmic accuracy, tempo, intonation, bowing, technique, style, and expression. Encourage your children to repeat previously learned music in a new more accomplished way, rather than allowing the repetitions of previously learned music to become a thoughtless exercise.

Finally, utilize the inherent characteristics in the music to motivate your children and to raise their level of performance. Have your children exaggerate the printed dynamic levels for more expression. Have them listen for beauty in their performance, not just technical details. Slow down the tempo of a piece that you're singing or studying to challenge your children to have more patience and discipline, while allowing them to hear the music in more detail and be able to correct subtle errors. Sustain a particular note to help your children listen more carefully to the intonation or tone quality of that note. Practice a section of a piece multiple times, each time changing something about it so the child will have a different focus and a new challenge with each playing. These and other instructional strategies that keep your child relaxed, and at the same time alert and focused, will prove to be very successful if you keep the standard of achievement set in the "stretch" position.

Have fun with music.

Host a "famous musicians" party, host a talent show for the neighborhood, play musical games, and be creative!

For a "famous musicians" party, get together with a parent or friend with musical training to plan a party in which all the guests are assigned an identity as a famous instrumentalist or vocalist. Send this information to them prior to the party, and ask them to find out something about the musician to share at the party, and then come to the party dressed up like that musician. Parents and children can participate together. Decide what music you want to perform. If you are creating a symphony of instrumentalists, ask the guests to imitate playing their musician's instrument — and be sure they're using correct hand position and posture (you can help them make adjustments after they arrive). Once the party begins, choose a conductor, put on a recording of the music, and have a rehearsal. Make decisions during the rehearsal what parts should be louder, what should be softer, and if some of the important instruments in a particular section should stand up. Decide who should be a soloist. Have everyone "hum" their parts as they gesture playing instruments, and be sure the conductor gives cues. After two or three rehearsals, take a break and have everyone share the information they found about their musician. Then turn on the video camera, and do the final performance. Make copies of the performance for all the guests.

A talent show can be performed by children of any age. Have your children decide what they want to perform, what they want to wear, have them design and create a stage area, send out invitations, plan and make refreshments, and perform their talent for the guests. If your children get stage fright, stand beside them to give them confidence, and even perform together with them if needed. Do this several times a year. Each performance will be highly motivating because of the concrete goal it provides, and with each experience your children will become more and more confident performing for an audience.

Musical games can take many forms, and are limited only by your imagination. Bounce balls to the beat of a recording or a drum; play "Simon Says" singing instead of speaking, having the followers imitate the leader's voice while they do what Simon says to do; play a communication game by singing the inflection of words you would normally be speaking—but without the words (pick a syllable like "ooh" or "wee"); clap "name rhythms" and "food rhythms" and have others try to guess the words that go with the sound of the claps; play "name that tune" by playing the first few notes of a recording and having each person write down the name of the tune on a piece of paper, then after doing ten or more tunes, see who got the most correct responses; the possibilities are endless! When you're creating ideas for games, get your children involved and help guide their ideas. Decide on the rules and parameters. Use the elements of rhythm, melody, harmony, dynamics, articulation, style, or tempo to make up your games — any one of these could be the basis for your games. Look for musical games on the web or in published materials, and, above all, have fun!

Get your extended family involved.

Nothing pleases grandparents more than seeing their grandchildren learning, growing, and enjoying life. And nothing brings families together like music. Have your children interview their grandparents, aunts, uncles, and cousins to find out what musical experiences they've had in their lifetimes. Ask them to tell their stories while your children record them on video or audiotape. And don't forget to have your children find out what kind of a musician you were as a growing child. Have your children compare what they find out from you about your experiences with their own. Some questions might be, "What age were you when you sang in church choir? Why did you decide to learn to play the tuba? What did your music teachers tell you about your potential to be a musician? Do you still have the cello you played on when you began lessons?" and so on. Through this process you will be building an interested audience for your children's musical activities, and you may uncover a well-hidden family secret through the process!

Record your family's musical activities.

Teach your children at a young age to operate a tape or CD recorder, and give them free use of it with and without your supervision. Giving them the use of a recorder is like putting a baby in front of a mirror to see and respond to her own image, but with sounds. This encourages great creativity, and some children will spend hours recording, rewinding, and replaying their creations. Ask them to share their favorites with the family.

Also, record your children's voices speaking, singing, and playing their instruments periodically as they grow, just as you record their height on a doorjamb or take videos of family activities. Label the recordings with the child's name and age, and replay them often. Congratulate your children on the progress they've made when you listen to old recordings.

Don't be apologetic if you lack formal musical training.

Many parents have a love of music but do not consider themselves musicians. If you fall into this category, you are an "amateur" in the literal sense — one who loves music. Stating that you're not a musician because you lack formal training, especially within earshot of your children, can cause them to begin to doubt your commitment, diminishing their confidence in you as the person responsible for their musical growth. If you are committed to musical training in your home, speak to your children and to others with confidence about your own passion. Your children will listen to you better than you want sometimes, and you want them to know how much you value the musical training you're providing. Be cautious about not talking negatively about your skills or insecurities as a musician. The great news is that, as your children grow as musicians, you will too!

Be your children's greatest cheerleader.

The impact you can have on your children's learning is powerful. Be sure it is positive and appropriately placed. You should encourage your children by praising them for specific accomplishments in a timely fashion. Be careful not to be too general in your praise. "That was good" is not nearly as effective or meaningful to a child as "I really liked how you made your voice get louder throughout the verse, just like the music says." An immediate praise response is best — the sooner the better after your child has done something that is praiseworthy.

Always be supportive for your children's attempts, even if the outcome is not always beautiful or moving. Encourage patience, and commend your children for demonstrations of good character while they're participating in musical activities. When they show respect for a sibling, they're willing to share, or they demonstrate patience, don't overlook these opportunities to show them your approval. Character development is a part of the whole musical education for your children. Be positive and consistent in telling them when they do well.

There are hundreds of ways you can help your children learn music at home. Give them the gift of your time and energy by brainstorming, designing, and creating effective and fun musical experiences for them. Make the commitment to follow through on your plans, and let your children help guide you in the process.

Private Instruction Options

Getting the aid of professionals, paired with support from home, is the best way to make the greatest strides in your child's musical achievement. If you've decided to get assistance outside your family to provide musical training for your children, many opportunities are available through private music organizations.

Community Programs

Your town will likely have programs where musical experiences are provided for your children. Here are some options to research in your area:

Church Programs — Children's choruses, praise bands, youth sing-alongs, and opportunities to perform in large ensembles are usually available. Most church programs will welcome you with open arms if they know you're interested in participating in music.

Local Bookstore — Authors and composers will often tour to bookstores around the country when they have new books and materials published. Some bookstores will present programs in conjunction with the visit of an author or composer in which children can sing, play instruments, read about music, and ask questions of the guest artist.

Local Music Store — Look for composers or performers to appear at your local music store, especially if they have recently published new materials. Some stores publish a newsletter that tells of their upcoming events. Get on the mailing list if you want to stay current with their events.

Community Chorus, Orchestra, and Band — In our town we have a children's chorus that is a high level performing group open to children only by audition. It is a performance opportunity for children of all ages who are highly skilled in music, and a significant participation fee is charged. Check into the opportunities in your area for community choruses, as well as orchestras and bands. Our community orchestra is a summer-only opportunity and is also open by audition only. Adults and high school students who pass the audition are welcome. No fee is charged. Our community band is also summer-only and open by audition only, but it is mostly adults. High school students are admitted only if they perform at a very high level. If they pass the audition, they earn a small income for performing. You may be surprised at how many groups you can find in your community that are open to children's participation. If none can be found, consider starting one!

YMCA/YWCA — Check these organizations for their musical offerings. Fees are usually quite reasonable and programs can include a wide range of options. Programs such as "vaudeville production" and "singing theater" may be offered, and some Y's will work together with other community organizations to offer Kindermusik, Suzuki, or Yamaha programs.

Youth Symphonies

Youth symphony programs abound in major metropolitan areas, and may also be available in smaller towns as well. Many of them not only cater to the advanced player, but also offer ensembles at intermediate and beginner levels. Most rehearse once or twice a week, and some offer special sectional rehearsals, music theory classes, and chamber music opportunities. Performances by the advanced groups often take place in professional symphony performance venues. For example, the Chicago Youth Symphony performs in Chicago's Symphony Center. It's an amazing experience for the members of the youth symphony to be able to perform on the same stage where so many great musicians have performed. Often, members of the parent symphony coach sectionals or ensemble rehearsals. There also are charity components to some of these organizations, in which smaller groups of student musicians perform at nursing homes, hospitals, and other community venues. Having these experiences will impact your children for the whole of their lives. Most youth symphonies have audition and entrance fees, and you may be required to purchase a number of tickets for their performances. Some groups travel on domestic or world tours.

Music Schools

Look for music schools in your area for private and group instruction to develop vocal and instrumental music skills, and

to learn music theory, ear training, rhythm instruction, movement and dance. Some of the types of schools you may find are:

Private Studios — Private teachers offer lessons in voice and
various instruments. They may teach in their homes, rent
space in a studio, or teach at a local school or church. Some may
even come to your home to teach. They may occasionally organize small groups of their students into ensembles for rehearsals and performances, and most teachers have a recital for their
students once or twice a year. Some studios have many teachers,
so be sure to find out what you can about the individual teacher
you're interested in before making a commitment. You may
want to have a sample lesson to find out what lessons would
be like, or at least ask the teacher's permission to observe a few
lessons. Your choice of teacher is a critical component of your
children's success. Most teachers charge tuition by the month
or by the semester.

Kindermusik Programs — Kindermusik programs are designed
for newborns to age seven. At the beginning level, parents and
babies participate in musical activities that stimulate social,
emotional, physical, and language development, and nurture
bonding between baby and parent. As the child grows, developmentally appropriate activities are incorporated into the lessons. The principles of child psychologists Piaget, Montessori,
Brazleton, Greenspan and Vvogtsky are at the foundation of
these activities. Kindermusik subscribes to the belief that the
parent is the child's best teacher, and although the activities
are scientifically based, they should also be great fun for both
children and parents. Look for teachers who are members of
the KEA (Kindermusik Educator's Association), and be sure to
observe classes before deciding to sign up.

Yamaha Programs — Piano and basic music instruction is the content of Yamaha Music Education programs. Children ages 3 to 8 are the focus, and comprehensive musicianship is the goal. Yamaha courses began in the mid-1950's in Japan by the president of the Yamaha Corporation to teach customers how to use the products they were producing. The Yamaha Music Foundation was established in 1966 to promote music education and international music activities. Children sing, do ear training, movement, and rhythm activities, learn music notation, and learn to play piano. Teacher certification, membership in MTNA (Music Teachers National Association), and other credentials should be checked before choosing to participate in a Yamaha program. Check with your local program for information about fees and lessons.

Suzuki Programs — Violin, viola, cello, double bass, flute, harp, guitar, and piano can be learned in Suzuki programs across the country. Programs generally accept children at age 5, and even earlier in some programs if the child can demonstrate the ability to focus and follow directions. The process for learning in Suzuki programs is the "mother-tongue" approach. Just as a parent teaches a child to speak, the parent becomes the teacher of the instrument. Characteristics of Suzuki programs are: every child can learn, parents serve as the daily teachers, listening and repetition are required for mastery, encouragement and loving support are important to the child's development, children learn in private and group lessons, repertoire is designed to provide technical challenges as well as a medium for expression, and children learn to read music only after they have established solid playing skills.

In America today many programs do not expect parents to learn to play the instrument, but only to attend lessons and learn how to monitor their children's practicing and progress. Programs typically offer one private and one group lesson each week. Group lessons are necessary to develop socialization, cooperation, and ensemble playing skills, and are for the purpose of repeating and reviewing material previously learned. Regular recitals and concerts are integral to these programs. Many Suzuki programs are housed at colleges or universities, and some are held in churches or in private studios. Look for teachers who have been certified through SAA (Suzuki Association of the Americas).

Local Music Stores — Local music store personnel can be very helpful to you in selecting an instrument for rental or purchase, and in providing private and group lessons. It can be very convenient, depending on its proximity to your home, and when you need to purchase music, reeds, or strings. They are immediately available to you. Just as with any other music studio, ask for a sample lesson or visit a lesson being taught in the store studio before making a commitment. Also, ask about group lessons, recitals, and ensemble experiences they may offer.

Summer Camps

Camp settings provide intensive musical training for your children at all levels. The length of camps ranges from one to eight weeks, and depending on your children's age, parents may also participate in lessons and programs during the course of the camp. Children will play their instruments as many as 8 hours a day at a summer music camp.

Even if your child has never had music lessons, some camps will start beginners. My son had his first cello lessons at the age of five at the American Suzuki Institute at Stevens Point, Wisconsin. At the camp he received two lessons a day from a master teacher for seven days, enjoyed the socialization of the other children both in and outside of his lessons, and performed in the final concert of the camp after just seven days of instruction. The camp had a profound and lasting effect on him, and it was a great way to get him started in formal lessons. We continued to attend summer camps for many years after this experience, mostly because he enthusiastically asked to go every year. Check colleges and universities in your area, ask your private teachers, look for listings of camps through Kindermusik, Yamaha, and Suzuki programs, and network with other parents to find quality camp programs for your children.

Homeschool Groups

As a homeschooler you may already have a network of parents who homeschool their children, and you may participate in organized groups for specific non-music learning opportunities. Start a conversation with those parents to find families interested in music, and create music groups for your children.

One of the families in our area developed a "Music Ambassadors" program, encouraging their children to take the responsibility of creating small groups of musicians to perform at local nursing homes and hospitals in groups of two to ten players or singers. After a few performances the children became well known at these homes, and the residents began to look forward to the mini-concerts at various times in the year. The children learned how to organize themselves, select music, choose practice time, lead rehearsals, and introduce their concerts, speaking to the audiences as they would introduce each "act." The wonderful reward for their labors was the warm reception they received by the residents. Eventually, they incorporated a "talk time" after the performances so they could get to know the residents, and they have developed ongoing relationships with them.

You can organize choirs, bands, or orchestras, designing musical opportunities for your children based on the skills and needs of the people in your groups. You may want to limit your goals to having occasional performances, or you may want to meet daily or weekly for lessons and rehearsals. Pool your resources to bring in special guest artists or teachers to meet with your children, or go out to experience a concert or special artist performing near you. Set up a "Practice Buddy" program having older children practice together with younger children. Give older children responsibility to teach specific techniques to younger children, and encourage them to think about the tools they will need to use as they analyze the skills of their budding students. Set up partnerships with the library, a church, the YMCA, or other community groups that may be willing to offer you the space you need, as well as other resources such as chairs, music stands, and a podium. The possibilities are endless!

College and University Programs

Many colleges offer pre-college "preparatory" lessons in music taught by the university faculty, graduate students, undergraduates, or independently contracted teachers. Private lessons, jazz programs, chamber music, theory lessons, piano classes, large ensembles, recitals, and competitions are some of the offerings you may find. Music Education programs seeking "field experiences" for their soon-to-be-educators are good resources. Contact your nearest college or university and inquire about the possibilities of connecting with these students.

The American String Teachers Association supports string projects at universities across the country to help alleviate the string teacher shortage in our country and encourage string players to become string teachers. The projects also provide the opportunity for children to study string instruments. The original model for these projects is at the University of South Carolina in Columbia, and there are programs at approximately 35 other colleges and universities nationwide. Classes for eight year olds through high school age students are offered at beginner, intermediate, and advanced levels. Private lessons, small ensembles, chamber music, theory classes, and Suzuki lessons are offered, as well as various levels of orchestras. They are taught by undergraduate students under the supervision of a Master Teacher, a Graduate Assistant, and/or a Director of the Project. Many projects are supported by private funding sources, and often fees are kept low in order to enable economically disadvantaged children to enroll.

Competitions

Local, regional, and national organizations sponsor competitions for music students. Requirements and age categories vary by the organization, and prizes include monetary awards, sponsorship to a camp, scholarships, opportunities to solo with a band, choir, or orchestra, and performing in a recital. Some national organizations that sponsor music competitions are: SAM (Society of American Musicians), MENC (Music Educators National Conference), ACDA (American Choral Directors Association), MTNA (Music Teachers National Association, ASTA (American String Teachers Association), Sphinx Organization, Fischoff Chamber Music Competition, and BOA (Bands of America). Community bands, symphony orchestras, community or church choirs, and musician's clubs may sponsor local and regional competitions.

Competition categories include not only solo performances, but also musical compositions, music technology, alternative style music, student conducting, and chamber music. Some also include an academic written-test component.

Adult Instruction

If you have been inspired to seriously study an instrument or voice, most of the previously listed private organizations also have an adult component. Additionally, many communities have adult amateur ensembles — bands, choirs, and orchestras — that would be delighted to have you participate.

Public Music Options

Becoming involved in public music activities can offer you some very low-cost, high-quality options for instruction.

Local Library Programs

Libraries that offer children's literary programs such as storytelling and theater may incorporate music into their offerings. Look for musical puppet shows, children's musical theater, sing-alongs, musical guest artists, and other music events. Our local library provides "Homeschool Support Services" that includes story times and monthly book discussions, and they provide services to help you find music recordings, do internet research about music, and find videos on musical topics. At Thanksgiving, our library sponsors performances by musical groups from all over the area to attract people into the library and kick-off the holiday season. Look for similar programs at your library, and consider participating!

Park District and Community College Offerings

Check your local park district and community college for music offerings. These organizations provide enrichment programs for your area, and you can enroll in courses that satisfy your interests, ranging from basket weaving to a complex college level math course for credit. Also, some of the best facilities in your community can be found in these venues. The music offerings can include guitar lessons, piano lessons, voice lessons, music technology, music and movement, and music appreciation. Be sure to make a long-term commitment, though, especially when learning to sing or learning an instrument. Many of these programs are limited to a summer, a quarter, or a semester at a time. Participating in a short program will not gain your children the high-level results proven by the long-term study of music.

Public School Music Programs

The Music Educators National Conference has published a paper on "Homeschooled Students' Participation in Public School Music Education," outlining their position, concerns, and the role of the music educator in working with homeschoolers. In the paper, MENC offers guidelines to educators and school districts on principles for setting up a good working relationship. With homeschooling dramatically increasing in the country, MENC maintains that,

> "while it [MENC] is neither "for" nor "against" homeschooling, adequate music education resources should be available to all students, regardless of how children obtain their education."[1]

A major concern of public schools, however, is that while parents of homeschooled children are tax payers and support public school facilities, faculty, staff, and instructional materials, the states in which districts receive funds for education based on enrollments cannot count homeschooled children in their enrollments.

"If the number of homeschooled children requesting public school services increases significantly, funding issues will need to be addressed by all who are affected by them."[2]

Also, MENC states the possible consequences of these issues:

"Unfortunately, because of these issues, or because of a philosophical reluctance by some school districts to cooperate with homeschoolers, an "us against them" atmosphere has been fostered in some areas. Consequently, the families, the communities, and the children involved can miss out on an opportunity to create a positive, empowering relationship."[3]

The good news is that public school music educators want to have inquisitive, talented children in their programs who are willing to work hard and be in attendance for all the required elements of the program. Some may even be seeking homeschoolers to participate in their programs in order to increase the size and quality of their performing groups. If you and your child are able to fulfill the requirements of the public school program and the district is open to having you participate, your child and the school program can both greatly benefit.

At my public high school I have been asked on several occasions to allow homeschoolers to participate in my orchestra program. I met with the families and explained that I would require everything of their children that I require of the students enrolled in the high school. I discussed the school and district policies with them (i.e.: rules for entering the building, my office hours, who they should contact in case of absence, etc.), and I gave them information about our state's Music Educators

Association District and All-State Festivals, local youth symphonies, summer camps, and other programs that I always
bring to the attention of my students. Some of the groups at
the school have limited membership, such as participation in
jazz band, pit orchestra, or string quartet, so I explained my
policies about auditions for these groups. I auditioned the
students, placed them in the appropriate orchestra, and when
school started I introduced these students to the others just as
I would introduce a student who just moved into the district. In
each case, the homeschooled students were warmly welcomed
and quickly incorporated as regular members of our school and
music community.

One homeschool family in Arizona, however, did not have
such success attempting to enroll their son in public school
band. As an elementary student, he was welcomed to participate in band lessons, rehearsals, and performances at their
local elementary school. He excelled on trumpet, and his
teacher highly recommended him for participation in middle
school band. However, while lessons had only been two times
per week in elementary school, the middle school required
enrollment in two classes per day, expecting daily attendance.
The family has five children who homeschooled through high
school, and all are very athletic and active in many areas. Making the commitment to transport one of their children to and
from the middle school for two classes every day was more of a
commitment than they were able to make, resulting in the family taking their son out of the school program (for the rest of
the story see Chapter 4, Family #4).

Homeschool parents should contact public school administrators to dialog about the opportunities that are available for
participation in public school programs. If protocols have been
set in the district and the school, they will be able to tell you

what your options are. If this request is new to them, you may need to be a pioneer and lay some groundwork. Check your state's policies, and look on the MENC website (<www.menc. org>) for the complete list of guidelines to music educators for offering public school music services to homeschooled children. The MENC guidelines are also reproduced in their entirety in Chapter 3 of this book.

3

Organizations That Offer Support

|||||||||||||||||||||||||||||||||||||||||||||||||||||||||||||||||||||||||||||||||||||||||||||

You should never feel like you're blazing a new trail when look-ing for support in your efforts to find music opportunities for your homeschooled children. There are numerous organizations willing to assist you as you seek information and advice.

MENC, the Music Educators National Conference, is the largest arts education professional association in the world with a membership of over 75,000 active, retired, and pre-service teachers. It is the only association that addresses all aspects of music education, serving millions of students nationwide. MENC addresses issues related to band, chorus, orchestra, general music, and jazz. It also has divisions for higher education, administration, research, and future teach-ers, and it addresses effective communication with parents, businesses, and the press.

Publications explaining and supporting the national stan-dards for the arts and music, as listed below, are available from MENC. Write to MENC Publications Sales, 1806 Robert Fulton

Drive, Reston, VA 20191. Credit card holders may call 800-828-0229, or order online at <www.menc.org>.

Standards Publications: The Arts

"National Standards for Arts Education: What Every Young American Should Know and Be Able to Do in the Arts." Content and achievement standards for dance, music, theatre, and visual arts; grades K-12. Reston, VA: Music Educators National Conference, 1994. Stock # 1605. ISBN 1-56545- 036-1.

"Perspectives on Implementation: Arts Education Standards for America's Students." A discussion of the issues related to implementation of the standards and of strategies for key constituencies that need to be involved in the process. Reston, VA: Music Educators National Conference, 1994. Stock #1622. ISBN 1-56545-042-6.

"The Vision for Arts Education in the 21st Century." The ideas and ideals behind the development of the National Standards for Arts Education. Reston, VA: Music Educators National Conference, 1994. Stock #1617. ISBN 1-56545-025-6.

Standards Publications: Music

"The School Music Program: A New Vision." The K-12 National Standards, PreK standards, and what they mean to music educators. Reston, VA: Music Educators National Conference, 1994. Stock #1618. ISBN 1-56545-039-6.

"Opportunity-to-Learn Standards for Music Instruction: Grades PreK-12." Information on what schools should provide in terms of curriculum and scheduling, staffing, materials and equipment, and facilities. Reston, VA: Music Educators National Conference, 1994. Stock #1619. ISBN 1- 56545-040-X.

"Performance Standards for Music: Strategies and Benchmarks for Assessing Progress Toward the National Standards, Grades PreK - 12." Sample assessment strategies and descriptions of student responses at the basic, proficient, and advanced levels for each achievement standard in the National Standards. Reston, VA: Music Educators National Conference, 1966. Stock #1633. ISBN 1-56545-099-X.

The MENC position paper on homeschooled students' participation in public school music, reprinted here, offers guidelines for homeschoolers and music educators. Following the position paper is a list of organizations that can offer you more information and assistance. Many listed are Illinois organizations, since that is my state. Look for similar organizations in your state.

MENC Position Paper

Homeschooled [1] Students' Participation in Public School Music Education

Position
A dramatic increase has taken place in homeschooling in the United States over the past twenty years. While aware of this increase, MENC is neither "for" nor "against" homeschooling. Whether children receive their education in a public, private, or parochial school, or at home, music education remains a core

subject, and MENC maintains that adequate music education resources should be available to all students, regardless of how children obtain their education.

Concerns

Homeschooling became lawful in all 50 states by 1993. By 2003, about two million students were being homeschooled, and the number of children being homeschooled in the United States continues to grow with every academic year. Homeschooling parents across the country represent all income brackets, education levels, races, and political and religious affiliations, and every state has at least one homeschooling association. Several states have begun to develop regional associations, and there are now several national homeschooling organizations.

In some states, education is still mainly controlled at the local school district level, while in others, policy applies to all districts in the state. Depending on the state, homeschoolers may be treated as a private school or as some other category, neither public school nor private school. The federal government has determined that each state must make its own rules, so there are no all-encompassing laws for homeschooled students.

In recent years, more students who are not enrolled in public school want access to public school resources, activities, and classrooms, especially in the areas of the arts, sports, and advanced math and sciences. As a result, schools are increasingly obliged to rethink the boundaries of public education.

Parents of homeschooled children argue that their tax dollars help pay for public school facilities, faculty, staff, and instructional materials, as well as curricular and extracurricular programs such as music instruction. This can be an additional point of contention. In some states, districts receive funds for education based on district enrollments that are then divided into site allotments. Although their parents pay taxes, homeschooled children are not counted in enrollments. If the numbers of homeschooled children requesting public school services increase significantly, funding issues will need to be addressed by all who are affected by them.

Currently, homeschoolers' participation in music education is affected by three issues: whether the district is required to provide the service, the problem of how to determine student eligibility, and the creation of a financial burden for the district. In addition, issues arise regarding performance requirements for participation in extracurricular and co-curricular activities and about priority for enrollment due to limited space and availability of classes, activities, and materials.

Unfortunately, because of these issues, or because of a philosophical reluctance by some school districts to cooperate with homeschoolers, an "us against them" atmosphere has been fostered in some areas. Consequently, the families, the communities, and the children involved can miss out on an opportunity to create a positive, empowering relationship.

The Music Educator's Role
Participation in curricular or extracurricular programs by homeschooled students is determined by state and local school district policy, and policies vary from district to district. Within these limits, the music educator's role is to maintain positive working relationships with all involved. This effort does not, however, assume that the question of how music education is provided remains unaddressed. Homeschooling is not a music educator's business, but music education is, regardless of where it takes place.

Whether the concerns are practical or philosophical, music educators are encouraged to take a position of neutrality except when it comes to the right of every child to receive a music education. Serving in this capacity demands tact and sensitivity. Teachers are advised to model the same skills and behaviors that form the heart of character education: trustworthiness, respect, responsibility, fairness, caring, and citizenship.

Guidelines
If homeschooling is unavailable:

- Be mentally prepared for the possibility that homeschooling may become available to parents in your district.

- Remind decision makers that music education is a core subject and should be included in every child's curriculum.

- Take the time now to explore ways that will improve your music program's capability to meet all students' needs. Consider emphasizing the advantages qualified music specialists offer to every child in any educational setting.

If homeschooling is available:

- Let homeschooling parents know, in writing, the terms of district, residency, and registration requirements regarding student attendance and achievement. Emphasize the specific rules and regulations as outlined by the school district that are imperative for participation in public school music programs.

- Adopt minimum academic requirements for homeschoolers equivalent to those that conventional students must meet in order to participate in cocurricular music activities where such requirements exist.

- Work with administrators to develop a set of policies and practices for enrollment in classes with limited space and availability. If the school district allows homeschoolers to enroll as part-time students in order to participate in music classes, discuss how registration will work for popular classes that accommodate only a limited number of students.

- Consider working directly with homeschooling groups and organizations to determine local needs and design programs applicable to those groups and organizations that are open to a partnership.

- Look for opportunities to build more productive relationships with the homeschooling community.

Whether homeschooling is available or not:

- Emphasize the fact that adequate music education resources should be available to all students.

- Keep lines of communication open with administration, parents, school boards, and music faculty colleagues.

- Be aware of your district's policy on homeschoolers' participation in school-related activities and keep abreast of changes in policy.

- Be respectful but clear with parents about what participation in school programs will entail, letting them know what will be expected of them, and what obligations they will have to the school district. Also be sure they are aware of any rules and policies to which they must adhere.

- Make an effort to include families in school activities and decision-making processes when possible.

- Be aware, and communicate to all parties involved, that state associations may comprise affiliate local or regional music education chapters that have different protocols and rules for participation in local community ensembles, music festivals, and competitions. Each chapter may make its own rulings and decisions on student participation. Be able to provide your state association's website and contact information as a resource.

- Hold all students to the same standards for behavior, performance, attendance, grade requirements, standards for participation in extracurricular activities, and other classroom rules.[2]

Support Organizations for Music Education

Advocacy for Music Education

<www.menc.org/resources/
viewmusic-education-advocacy-central>
See also Support Music.Com, Music For All, and Dream Out Loud

America Sings!

<www.americasings.org>
A non-profit organization which creates massive, non-competitive choral music festivals featuring hundreds of school and community singing groups from across with United States. America Sings! is an MENC affiliated organization. For more information, e-mail info@americasings.org or call (800) 372-1222.

American Choral Directors Association

<acda.org>
The American Choral Directors Association (ACDA) is a non-profit music-education organization whose central purpose is to promote excellence in choral music through performance, composition, publication, research, and teaching. In addition, ACDA strives through arts advocacy to elevate choral music's position in American society.

The American Composers Forum

<www.composersforum.org>
The American Composers Forum links communities with composers and performers, encouraging the making, playing and enjoyment of new music. With 1,700 members and a wide variety of innovative and educational programs, the Forum has grown into one of the largest composer-service organizations in the United States. It currently has chapters in Boston, Los Angeles, Minneapolis/St. Paul, New York, Philadelphia, San Francisco, and Washington D.C. Contact Dr. Krystal Prime Banfield, Director of Education, American Composers Forum, 332 Minnesota Street, Suite #E145, Saint Paul, Minnesota 55101; (651) 251-2812.

American Guild of English Handbell Ringers, Inc.

<www.agehr.org>
AGEHR is dedicated to advancing the musical art of handbell/handchime ringing through education, community, and communication. The approximately 7,500 members, mostly directors of handbell/handchime choirs, seek to carry out the motto: "Uniting People through a Musical Art."

American Orff Schulwerk Association

<www.aosa.org>
Carl Orff was a composer and a music education visionary. Schulwerk, as envisioned by composer Carl Orff, is a way to teach and learn music and movement. Join AOSA for professional development, participation in a community of talented arts educators, and joyful discovery through music. Orff Schulwerk associations are active in more than 30 nations, worldwide.

American School Band Directors Association

<home.comcast.net/~asbda>
The American School Band Directors Association, Inc. is recognized as a wholesome constructive force in school instrumental music. ASBDA includes members in all fifty states and Canada totaling one thousand active and affiliate members, and a strong supporting group of associate members.

American String Teachers Association

<www.astaweb.com>
ASTA is a membership organization for string and orchestra teachers and players, helping them to develop and refine their careers. ASTA's members range from budding student teachers to artist-status performers. The organization provides a vast array of services, including instrument insurance, an award-winning scholarly journal, discounts on publications and resources, annual professional development opportunities, and access to a network of colleagues throughout the string profession.

Americans For The Arts

<www.artsusa.org>
Americans for the Arts is the nation's leading nonprofit organization for advancing the arts in America. With more than 40 years of service, they are dedicated to representing and serving local communities and creating opportunities for every American to participate in and appreciate all forms of the arts.

Arts Education Partnership

<www.aep-arts.org>
AEP is a national coalition of arts, education, business, philanthropic and government organizations that demonstrate and promote the essential role of the arts in the learning and development of every child and in the improvement of America's schools.

Association Of Illinois Music Schools

<www3.niu.edu/aims>
The purpose of the Association of Illinois Music Schools is to advance the cause of music in higher education generally and to improve the quality and program of the music educational system in Illinois through the promotion of cooperation between all colleges and universities and through the exercise of educational leadership.

Barbershop Harmony Society

<www.barbershop.org>
In alliance with other a cappella organizations worldwide, the Barbershop Harmony Society is committed to enriching lives in every generation and community through the

lifelong benefits of a cappella harmony singing. The Society is built on fundamental principles that drive our mission: that singing brings joy to our lives and world.

The Conductors Guild

<www.conductorsguild.org>
The Conductors Guild is the only music service organization devoted exclusively to the advancement of the art of conducting and to serving the artistic and professional needs of conductors. More than 1,850 members represent all fifty United States and more than thirty other countries.

The Early Childhood Music And Movement Association (ECMMA)

<www.ecmma.org>
ECMMA is an organization for professionals whose membership represents the entire range of early childhood music and movement, including school music teachers, studio teachers, music therapists, university methods instructors, researchers, and material/methodology providers. ECMMA seeks to promote best practices by facilitating networking amoung the diverse professions that make up early childhood music and movement. ECMMA publishes a quarterly journal, *Perspectives*, for all its members.

Grammy® In The Schools

<www.grammyintheschools.com>
This website is notable for a section on careers in music, a valuable resource to guide and direct aspiring musicians into the profession. The Grammy® Foundation also sponsors competitions, awards, camps, and master classes connecting students with artists and professionals in the music industry.

Homeschool Music Association

<www.homeschoolmusic.net>
The Home School Music Association, Inc., (HSMA) began in 1993 as an organization dedicated to meeting the music education needs of Christian home-schooled students. They currently offer Band, Choral, Orchestral, and Elementary Music programs. HSMA rehearses weekly in the greater Lansing, Michigan area.

Illinois Arts Alliance/Foundation

<www.artsalliance.org>
Since 1982, the Illinois Arts Alliance/Foundation (IAAF) has been Illinois' primary multidisciplinary arts service organization, strengthening the nonprofit arts in Illinois and enabling arts organizations to better serve their communities.

Illinois Arts Council

<www.state.il.us/agency/iac>
IAC is the official state agency that supports the arts through grant funding that provides a variety of community and educational arts services, including arts residencies in schools.

Illinois General Assembly

<www.ilga.gov>
Track bills related to the arts as they progress through committee, to the floor, and to the Governor's desk.

Illinois State Board Of Education

<www.isbe.state.il.us>
ISBE is the official state agency that develops the rules, regulations and procedures to implement education policy as

determined by the State Legislature. The site offers the latest developments in teaching standards, student learning standards and teacher recertification. A listing of employment opportunities is also included.

Kennedy Center For The Performing Arts

<www.artsedge.kennedy-center.org>
This website is designed to link arts and K-12 education through technology. Students can chat with artists online and the site provides teaching guides for dance, music and theatre performances at Kennedy Center in Washington, D.C.

Kindermusik® Educators Association

<www.utm.edu/staff/sholt/cwd/kea>
The KEA is a professional organization of early childhood music educators teaching the Kindermusik curricula. It is designed for children from birth to age seven.

MENC: The National Association For Music Education

<www.menc.org>
MENC (Music Educators National Conference), the largest arts education professional association in the world, is the national parent organization of IMEA (Illinois Music Educators Association), as well as the other state Music Educators Associations. MENC has a membership of over 75,000, and it is the only association that addresses all aspects of music education.

Music Teachers National Association

<www.mtna.org>
The mission of Music Teachers National Association is to advance the value of music study and music making to society and to support the professionalism of music teachers.

Musicfriends

<www.musicfriends.org>
MusicFriends is a group of parents, community members, and other music advocates working to support local school music programs through grassroots initiatives. It is sponsored by MENC.

National Association Of College Wind And Percussion Instructors

<www.nacwpi.org>
NACWPI's members include university, college, and conservatory teachers. It encourages the effective teaching of wind and percussion instruments on the college level; serves as a forum for information; and supports fine music and instruments in wind and percussion. NACWPI also coordinates activities with other groups and encourages the performance of solo and chamber music. NACWPI is an MENC affiliated organization; its national and division officers are members of MENC.

National Association Of Music Merchants

<www.namm.org>
NAMM®'s members represent every aspect of musical instrument manufacturing and retailing. Their mission is to unify, lead, and strengthen the global music products industry and to increase active participation in music making.

National Association For The Study And Performance Of African American Music

<www.naspaam.org>
The National Association for the Study and Performance of African American Music (NASPAAM) is an organization whose purpose is to further the development and

dissemination of African-American music through advocacy, education, and performance. The organization is committed to providing leadership and motivation for music educators, musicians, and others interested in fostering the inclusion of African and African-American music in education and society. The organization serves its members and others by increasing the awareness of Black Music and its contribution to the arts, culture, and society.

The Percussive Arts Society

<www.pas.org>
PAS is the largest percussion organization in the world with more than 8,000 members, and it is considered the central source for information and networking for percussionists and drummers of all ages and skill levels. Established in 1961, the society is dedicated to promoting percussion education, research, performance and appreciation throughout the world. PAS publishes *Percussive Notes* magazine and *Percussion News*. PAS also produces the annual Percussive Arts Society International Convention (PASIC), featuring more than 100 concerts, clinics, master classes, labs, workshops, panels and presentations, an indoor Marching Percussion Festival, and the Drum & Percussion Expo. PAS is headquartered at 110 W. Washington St., Suite A, Indianapolis, Indiana, 46204 (317/974-4488), and is home to the Percussive Arts Museum and Library, which contain rare and unusual percussion instruments and scores.

Sigma Alpha Iota International Music Fraternity

<sigmaalphaiota.org/home>
SAI's mission is to encourage, nurture and support the art of music. Founded in 1903, SAI has over 320 collegiate and alumnae chapters around the country, with more than

100,000 initiated members. SAI has been a pioneer in supporting music education, performance, and composition in colleges, communities, the nation, and the world. Through its foundation, Sigma Alpha Iota Philanthropies, Inc., assistance is given to the Kennedy Center, Brevard Music Center, Aspen, Round Top, and many other music facilities and programs.

Society Of American Musicians

<www.samusicians.com>
The Society of American Musicians was founded in 1914 with the intent of promoting the best interests of music in America, and maintaining the highest standards of musicianship. Through competition, awards, and performance opportunities, the Society offers assistance and encouragement to young musicians and promising artists.

Supportmusic

<www.supportmusic.com>
This site offers effective tips for taking action, and the latest evidence of music's importance. It is designed for parents, students, teachers, and anyone looking for ideas to support their music programs. It is sponsored by NAMM® and MENC.

Suzuki Association Of The Americas

<suzukiassociation.org>
The Suzuki Association of the Americas, Inc. is the not-for-profit organization officially licensed to support, guide and promote Suzuki education in North, Central and South America. They are a coalition of teachers, parents, educators, and others who are interested in making music education available to all children.

Sweet Adelines International

<www.sweetadelineintl.org>
Sweet Adelines is a worldwide organization of women singers committed to advancing the musical art form of barbershop harmony through education and performance.

Technology Institute For Music Educators

<www.ti-me.org>
The Technology Institute for Music Educators (TI:ME)
is a non-profit corporation registered in the State of
Pennsylvania whose mission is to assist music educators in
applying technology to improve teaching and learning in
music.

Ten - Golden Apple's Teaching Excellence Network

<www.goldenappleten.org>
Golden Apple's Teaching Excellence Network is a place to
create, experiment, debate, connect, and explore the world
of teaching with other excellent educators.

U.S. Department Of Education

<www.ed.gov>
This is the official US Government agency that implements
Federal education legislation including the No Child Left
Behind Act (NCLB). USDE also conducts research and pro-
vides various grant opportunities.

Additional Organizations

You also may want to check these organizations for your specific needs:

American Harp Society <www.harpsociety.org>
American Music Conference <www.amc-music.org>
American Society of Composers, Authors & Publishers
   <www.ascap.com>
American Viola Society <www.americanviolasociety.org>
Artists House Music <www.artistshousemusic.org>
Association for Technology in Music Instruction
   <atmionline.org>
Bands of America <www.bands.org>
Bluegrass Preservation Society, Inc.
   <www.bluegrasspreservation.org>
Chamber Music America <www.chamber-music.org>
Dream Out Loud - Advocacy Materials from the
   Chicago Symphony Orchestra
   <www.cso.org/main.taf?p=8,2,143,1>
Fiddler Magazine <www.fiddle.com>
Guitar Foundation of America <www.guitarfoundation.org>
International Clarinet Society <www.clarinet.org>
International Double Reed Society <www.idrs.org>
International Foundation for Music Research
   <www.music-research.org>
International Horn Society <www.hornsociety.org>
International Society of Bassists <www.isbworldoffice.com>
International Trombone Association <www.ita-web.org>
International Trumpet Guild <www.trumpetguild.org>
Internet Cello Society <www.cello.org>
John Philip Sousa Foundation <www.sousafoundation.org>
League of American Orchestras <www.americanorchestras.org>
Mariachi Heritage Society <www.mariachiheritagesociety.com>
Midwest International Band and Orchestra Clinic
   <www.midwestclinic.org>
Mr.Holland's Opus Foundation <www.mhopus.org>

Music for All <www.musicforall.org>
National Flute Association <www.nfaonline.org>
Opera for Everyone <www.operaforeveryone.com/mesite>
Support Music <supportmusic.com>
The Chicago Flute Club <www.chicagofluteclub.org>
The College Music Society <www.music.org>
The National Music Council <www.musiccouncil.org>
US Air Force Bands <www.usafband.af.mil>
US Air Force Heritage of America Band
   <www.heritageofamericaband.af.mil>
US Army Bands <bands.army.mil>
US Marine Bands <www.marineband.usmc.mil>
US Navy Bands <www.navyband.navy.mil>
Viola da Gamba Society <vdgsa.org>
Violin Society of America <www.vsa.to>

4

Advice From Homeschool Families

In my interviews with a number of homeschool families across the nation whose children are involved in music, the following themes surfaced repeatedly:

- Know your children—look for readiness, interest, and desire; know their natural abilities and find weaknesses that need extra encouragement

- Encourage your children in various ways—find ways to encourage them based on who they are and what motivates them

- Be willing to get involved and take responsibility for your children's learning—devote uninterrupted time to help your children practice; learn to play an instrument; set high expectations

- When you make a commitment, follow through on it—be sure to do what you say you're going to do; don't make false promises

- Find a quality teacher — find someone who fits your values and expectations, and who holds a high musical standard

- The final goal in music instruction is a lifelong love of music — let this principle guide the decisions you make for your children

Each family is unique and has put these themes into practice in different ways; each has chosen instructional strategies that have satisfied the needs and desires of all the members of the family; and all have been successful at teaching their children the love of music. At the end of each family story, they offer their advice on how you might make it work in your home.

Family #1

John and Joyce live in a suburb of Chicago. They have two children, ages 23 and 25. They homeschooled their oldest child from age nine to age fourteen, and their youngest from six to fourteen. Both parents are musical. John is an amateur musician who studied piano for several years and sings in church choir. Joyce has a bachelor's degree in music education, and while her children were growing up she taught voice and piano lessons. She also works with children's choirs at church for special worship services, and teaches music during Sunday school classes.

They believe music has been very important in the development of their children. On a scale of one to ten, they value music at an eight for their family (ten being the highest). When I asked Joyce what they'd done to encourage their children's participation in music, she listed numerous activities, including singing as a family, playing piano and singing together, arranging piano lessons for the children taught by their grandmother, and encouraging them as positively as they could.

John and Joyce believed very strongly that they did not want to be negative critics or struggle with their children to practice, and they worked diligently through their positive language and encouragement to prevent the feeling that music was a day-to-day "grind." At the same time, because Joyce was musically trained and could immediately hear when errors occurred in the children's practice sessions, she knew there were times when they needed help, so she would patiently sit with them at the piano, singing with them, and assisting them in correcting their mistakes. One of her goals was to encourage them to be independent musicians and take ownership of their musical education, so she would correct them only when they asked for or needed help. When recitals were on the horizon and the music needed extra preparation, Joyce would begin to work with them more regularly to help them get ready for the performance. Outside of that, though, she preferred to allow them to be accountable to the piano teacher, rather than to her standards or expectations.

Listening to a broad range of music was also a huge part of their household. Children's songs, Christian praise music, and classical music played constantly throughout their home, and they would visit the library regularly to choose new CD's. Once when their son was six years old, he chose a CD of Mozart's *The Magic Flute* to bring home. Joyce said to him, "I don't think this is what you want," thinking he might not know by the cover of the CD what it was, or that it might be beyond his understanding or enjoyment. But he insisted that it *was* what he wanted, and when he got it home he happily listened to it over and over again. To this day he loves to listen to this opera as much as any other piece of music!

When Joyce reflected on the decisions she and John had made for their children's musical training, she remembered many times when they had taken a musical direction or made a musical choice based on an interest or desire their children had expressed. As evidenced by *The Magic Flute* occurrence, she feels gratified that she was willing to listen to her children when they expressed their desires to her, and she's glad that she gave them opportunities to make choices. In many ways, she feels she has learned as much from her children as they have learned from her by following them down an unexpected pathway. She knows she and John made a wise choice to expose their children in their early years to many different types of music. As a result the children have learned to appreciate a variety of styles of music, and their enjoyment of music has taught them that music is worthy as a lifelong pursuit.

Joyce's advice for homeschool parents: "Your attitude will make a difference to your children. If everything you talk about and do is play sports, or go to church, then the children will learn that's what is important to you. If you ignore music your children will think it's not important. Learning music is not a fad, but core to the individual's development. It is important to expose your child to music at a young age. To become a good reader you must hear the language first. Hearing music is critical to your child learning music. Are you open to exposing your child to a variety of musical styles? Or do you only listen to one type? When the parent is single minded, the child falls in lockstep with the parent's ideals or rebels and goes the opposite direction. Celebrate variety by looking for recordings, playing them, using Orff instruments, participating in Kindermusik, looking for musical toys, using simple items in the home (banging on pots and pans, for example), and then begin to explore lessons on keyboard and other instruments, and sing.

"Look for support groups for your interests. Look for programs where children can write music and create music — like doing crafts with your kids — and record them making up songs. If music is a part of your life, it will become a part of theirs. Music teaches children *how* to learn, and that's a lifelong process."

Family #2

Ruth is a 25-year-old cellist who was homeschooled from sixth grade through high school. She has two younger sisters, ages 24 and 15. Her family moved frequently as she was growing up, so she had a variety of musical experiences at different stages of her development. Her family currently lives in a rural area in upstate New York.

Ruth recently completed her master's degree in cello performance. Her mother has a bachelor's degree in piano performance, and her father took piano lessons and sang in choir in college but doesn't participate in musical activities. Having married a musician, however, he has listened to practicing, recitals, and concerts and is quite knowledgeable about music. Ruth says her family considers music education a nine or ten out of ten.

Their home was filled with classical music for most of Ruth's childhood. At age six she began piano lessons, and a short time later her sister, Hannah, began to study violin. They studied at the "Neighborhood Music School" affiliated with Yale University, which was not far from their home at the time. Ruth also participated in music theory and music history classes offered by the school, and at age eleven she began cello lessons.

In choosing when to begin lessons for their daughters, Ruth's parents were keenly aware of the interests, level of commitment, and abilities of their children, and they made decisions for them based on that awareness. Ruth remembers her mother attempting to start her on piano lessons before the age of six, deciding she wasn't ready, and waiting several months before making a long-term commitment to lessons. When Ruth's sister begged to take violin lessons at five years of age, the parents waited again. Hannah asked repeatedly for six months to have violin lessons before her parents finally agreed to start her. At age eleven, Ruth went to a music school fundraiser where free one-time lessons were offered on instruments, and she became enamored with cello. She took a lesson, and decided she *had* to learn to play it. Again, her parents set the rules: "You may start learning cello, providing piano remains your primary focus." Of course, Ruth was willing to accept these conditions, but ultimately her love for cello won, and today she is an accomplished cellist.

Ruth's grandparents played an integral part of her musical interest by taking her to concerts and giving her gifts of CD's, books, and games about music. In 8th and 9th grades Ruth participated in the Youth Orchestra in her area, and because she had become so capable of reading music from her piano experience, she enjoyed success at learning quickly on cello. Then her family moved out of the metropolitan area where they had been able to take advantage of so many musical opportunities, into a more rural setting where they had fewer choices. It was a challenge to find high quality musical experiences for both girls. They found a teacher for Ruth that required a 75-minute commute each way for lessons. This commute was difficult for the family, but then Hannah enrolled with a teacher that was even farther away. They found themselves traveling two hours each way for lessons. It was a blessing to the parents when Ruth and Hannah got their driver's licenses and they could drive to their lessons without their parents having to take them.

Moving to a rural area turned out to be a wonderful thing for Ruth. While she expected to have difficulty finding quality musical experiences, she actually found something even better than her youth symphony and lessons in the large metropolitan area she had left. The local symphony was looking for string players, and they asked her to play. The membership of the orchestra was mostly adults, some of whom were very accomplished, and Ruth enjoyed their mentorship, growing greatly in that environment. The schedule also was a better fit for Ruth and her family, and she progressed very quickly.

Ruth's advice: "Look for good teachers at universities or colleges. Ask for recommendations of teachers from people you know and trust, and look for successes in the programs. If things aren't working out, be willing to make the tough decision to change teachers. The quality of your teacher can make all the difference in your success. Finally, know your priorities for your children, and make decisions based on what you know is best for them."

Family #3

Laura has two children — a thirteen year old son and a nine year old daughter. Her son has always homeschooled, and they will soon be deciding whether he will go to public high school. Her daughter has homeschooled for two years. Laura and her husband are enthusiastic amateur musicians who sing in their church choir. Laura also played flute in college. On a scale of one to ten, music is a nine or ten in their priorities.

When their children were born they were immersed in classical music in their home through the playing of recordings, and as infants and toddlers they attended many of their parents choir rehearsals. Both children participated in

Kindermusik and Orff classes through the nearby university, and also at their park district and a local music school. One day when their daughter was attending class at the music school, their son wandered into the studio of a piano teacher who was practicing. The two struck up a conversation and immediately hit it off. The parents decided to enroll their son in piano lessons with this teacher, and the relationship between teacher and pupil to this day has been wonderfully successful. Both children also became involved in the children's choirs in their area, and they have met with great success. As a result of their early training they both were able to pass vocal auditions to participate in select vocal ensembles, singing in parts, in other languages, and even being chosen to sing a solo with a select group. Their son has joined an instrumental ensemble in which he plays recorder and piano, and he has found great joy in participating in this ensemble.

When her son was seven years old, Laura, having spent so much time at the music school, noticed an advertisement for office help at the school. She answered the ad, got the job, and now volunteers her time in exchange for lessons for her children. She calls it a "win-win" situation, benefiting both her children and the school.

When I asked Laura if she had encountered any problems, she said that coming to terms with the purpose of music lessons was the most important decision they had to make as parents. If your purpose is to develop an accomplished performer, for example, you may choose to do things differently than if your purpose is to foster a love for music. This purpose affects what you expect from practice sessions and how you deal with issues that arise as the children are learning and growing. For example, their son, who was very creative from the earliest lessons, would make tunes up on the piano while he was practicing. This became his form of self-expression, and he would communicate more clearly through playing piano than verbally. "When he was mad you could really hear it!" she said. She didn't want him to lose his enjoyment of music by telling him to practice only what the teacher wanted him to practice, so she allowed him much freedom in deciding what and how to practice. "The practice police didn't always show up at our house," she mused. She thinks his current enthusiasm and love for music is a result of this attitude that she and her husband held when he was younger.

Advice from Laura: "In finding the right teacher, I would recommend interviewing a couple teachers to find out why they teach. Some teachers teach because they love it, and some teach for the results — to show off their students and win competitions. Take a trial lesson and don't commit to a semester until you're certain you have a good fit with your beliefs and needs. Most teachers are open to doing sample lessons if you ask for them. The world of music is small. If you know a musician you trust, that person can recommend someone who might be good for your child.

"It's helpful for you to have an idea of what you want for your child. Our daughter is nine years old and very smart but she has trouble reading, and reading music is frustrating to her. She's in music for an entirely different reason than our son. For her the benefit is not so much self-expression, but the process of learning music to improve her reading skills. We've set up schedules for practicing so the children are not listening to each other's practicing, and we discourage our son from playing out of our daughter's piano books. This way she can remain focused on the process of reading, and not be frustrated that she can't play the pieces as well as he can with so much less effort. You should set up an agenda that you know is best for your children.

Rigidity is to be avoided. Be as honest with yourself as you can about why you want your children to learn music."

Family #4

Steve and Annette live in Scottsdale, Arizona and have five children, all of whom were homeschooled from Kindergarten through high school. Steve played piano and French horn through childhood and later added guitar as well. Annette was a Voice Performance major in college, also having participated in school drama and music programs throughout her youth. When their first child was four years old they decided to homeschool and enjoyed it so much they continued with their four other children. Their home was filled with a wide variety of music and musical entertainment. Steve and Annette felt it was critical to identify each of their children's personalities, gifts, and talents so they could guide them to participate in activities in which they would find success and enjoyment.

Their eldest enjoyed the challenge that Boy Scouts presented; their second had a passion for horseback riding; their third, music; their fourth, sports (predominantly baseball); and their fifth, dancing. Even though a couple of their children played the piano, it was their third child, Roy, who most fully embraced music.

Roy started playing piano at age seven, and at ten expressed an interest in learning to play the trumpet. Steve and Annette called the elementary school within walking distance to their home and spoke with the band teacher. He met with Roy privately several times and then invited him to participate in the school band. Roy was inspired by this teacher, and very little prodding was necessary for him to practice and excel. He played with this band for three years. During his sixth grade year, the band teacher formed a jazz band comprised of the best musicians from three different elementary schools. Roy was selected, and the group even won some local competitions.

While his elementary school music experience was relatively agreeable and encouraging, the middle-school (seventh and eighth grade) music program was not so accommodating. As a homeschooler, the district policy regarding band class participation required him to be enrolled in at least two classes at the school, and attend school every day. This arrangement would have been too much of an interruption to their daily homeschool schedule and would have been a difficult commitment to juggle while still schooling four other children. Annette discovered through a friend that a nearby high school had formed a band for the best musicians recruited from the various middle schools in the district. Roy auditioned for the director and was invited to join this band which met one afternoon each week and performed two concerts each semester — a schedule much more accommodating for their family. Roy played with this band for two years until he reached high school age.

The district rule of requiring enrollment in two classes was still enforced for homeschooled students who wanted to participate in the high school music program, so the family searched for yet another option. They found a wonderful solution at a local community college that had an award winning community band. The band rehearsed one evening each week and performed two concerts each semester. Roy auditioned and was warmly invited into the band as the youngest member they'd ever had. Many of the musicians had been playing their instruments for over thirty years. He participated with this band for two years and found it to be a fertile learning environment full of encouragement and enthusiasm.

While still in high school Roy also got together with a local division of the Disabled American Veterans (DAV). Once each week he would play his bugle at the local National Cemetery as a member of the DAV ritual team for graveside services. His playing replaced a recorded version of "Taps," and he received many tearful thanks from the families who attended those services. Sharing his musical talent with these disabled veterans was yet another enriching experience for Roy.

Annette's advice: "Do what is best for your family. We carefully weigh our obligations and only commit to those that we know we can carry out. When the middle school insisted that Roy be enrolled in two classes and attend every day, we knew it wouldn't work for our family. We kept searching and found a more suitable situation for his musical advancement. We say, "Never Give Up!"

"Not every child should be involved in music as a matter of course. Discover your child's talents and guide them to where they can be successful. Find those activities that best fit your family's lifestyle."

Family #5

Karen and her husband have three children, ages sixteen, twelve, and ten. They have homeschooled their children from the beginning of their schooling to the present time. Karen grew up as a vocalist, singing jazz in school groups and listening mainly to jazz. Her husband is a self-taught guitarist. Both have had minimal formal training in music.

Music is played much of the time in their home. The whole family listens to a wide variety of music, and both parents consider it a high priority to pass on the love of music to their children. "It's who we are," said Karen. "It's imperative in our home. We require them to do music, not just to put on a résumé or to check it off of a list of things all good parents should do. We want our children to develop their own love of music and to have a passion for it. We don't want them to do it just because we want them to."

All three children have been enrolled in Suzuki lessons from the age of six, and two are currently continuing to study. They participate in private lessons, group lessons, summer camps, and chamber music. They also take classes in music history, music theory, singing, and performing arts (including choir, dancing, and speaking).

Karen believes that her children's extensive experience with music has made them more confident individuals. "They have been performing in various ways since the age of four, and this has really built their confidence," she said. Karen believes that, with this variety of experiences, they excel in social situations because they're accustomed to dealing with adults and all ages of children, which puts them at an advantage over other children who haven't had these experiences.

Karen's advice: "Great teachers = great results! Find the best teachers you can. This will save you a lot of wasted time and angst. When things get difficult, bribe your children. Pay them for tedious jobs and difficult practicing that are well done. Get into a practice routine, and look to the music teacher for guidance on how to practice with your children. Find situations where your children can be inspired and their interest in music can be renewed, such as going to professional concerts, attending camps, etc. Don't underestimate the importance of the inspiration a good teacher can provide!

"Find a parent mentor who has children involved in music. An acquaintance of mine became my mentor and I regularly asked for her advice. Also, our children's teachers guided us in choosing appropriate experiences. After getting the advice, we made decisions that we knew were best for our family. Music learning has an ebb and flow just like learning in other areas; there are times when we're really focused and times when we've been more relaxed. It's important to know your children and what they need when. At age eleven our son learned the Boccherini Cello Concerto, a long and difficult piece of music for a child that age. At the point when he completed learning it, we decided that it was time to pull back because it had become overwhelming, and to this day he has not ever performed that piece. We went on to other things that were more appropriate for him at the time. We constantly monitor and adjust our expectations of him.

"My daughter amazes me at what she's accomplished through discipline and hard work. She has some difficulty with fine motor skills, and I think she appreciates what she's accomplished even more than my son who had things come much more easily. The students who sit at the back of the orchestra have a passion for music because they have to work hard to achieve. They are the ones who continue music for a lifetime.

"Have your children pay for some of their musical experiences. We had our children pay part of their way to music camp. This has taught them responsibility, and they've grown to have a sense of ownership in their learning, not one of entitlement.

"I would recommend that parents enroll their children in movement or early childhood music classes, and then start lessons on an instrument when they're ready. When they can physically read is a good indicator of readiness. Expose them to a lot of different things, and above all teach them to enjoy music."

Family #6

This family has five children, all of whom have participated in music. They have homeschooled from the beginning of their schooling through the end of middle school, and they all have attended public high school. Neither the mother nor the father have had any formal training in music, and they regret not having music in their background. As a result, they have encouraged their children's participation in music. Their approach to music instruction for their children has been low-key. They believe that music experiences should be for their children's fun and enjoyment, and they have done what they could to avoid the negative stigma some music instruction carries. On a scale of one to ten, they place music as "at least an eight."

All five children had early music lessons. They studied viola, guitar, and piano, and two participated in their high school orchestras. During their middle school years, the children participated in their local public school programs, including jazz band and orchestra. They also sang in church choir and performed on their instruments in church. They found private teachers by networking with other people who were involved in music, and they went to the local music store for guitar lessons.

Advice from Family #6: "Since we are musically illiterate, we didn't realize that one of our children's teachers wasn't pushing him hard enough. It took us some time to figure this out and we didn't have any help in discovering this. We just realized that we weren't seeing much progress over a long period of time. My recommendation is that when you don't see progress, or you sense a negative vibe from your children, you should investigate other options for their musical instruction, including possibly changing teachers."

Family #7

Janet has two children, ages fifteen and nine. Rebecca, the fifteen year old, homeschooled for two years while in middle school, and her nine year old brother is in a public school. He is an extreme extrovert and resists being taught. He is very strong-willed, and learns much better through self-discovery. He taught himself to read, and has learned many skills on his own. Rebecca is a quiet late bloomer and works hard to please her teachers.

Janet studied piano as a child but does not consider herself a proficient player. She loves to listen to music, and she appreciates and respects it. Her husband is a non-musician who pays the bills and attends some of the children's programs. He is very appreciative of the commitment involved in learning music, and he is very proud of them when he attends his children's performances.

The children began Suzuki lessons with a teacher they found by the recommendation of a friend. Rebecca's studies on cello have given her much to celebrate. Her development was slow as a young child, and the cello lessons improved her ability to socialize and to become more verbally competent. Rebecca became a homeschooler only after her parents met other homeschoolers in their cello Suzuki program, who told them of the benefits they had reaped with their own children. When Rebecca was in seventh grade, her parents decided to take the plunge, and made the commitment to homeschool her for two years. Her mother says that if she had known how beneficial it would have been to homeschool Rebecca she would have started much earlier. Rebecca is now back in public school, having just finished her freshman year in high school. She is a high achieving student academically and she excels in the school's orchestra. She continues to take cello lessons, participate in summer music camps, and play in the local community youth orchestra.

Janet's advice: "I believe the value of studying music is a ten. Studying music not only develops musical skills, but character as well. It develops every aspect of the person. Teach your children music even at the expense of other subjects. They can always catch up in other areas, but music has a long learning curve and must be started early. It also has wonderful healing properties.

"I wish I'd started my children earlier in piano lessons. I had no idea what music lessons were going to mean to my daughter and what world I was walking into when we started. This isn't Kansas, where you open the door and everything's in color. I didn't know very much, and I had to experience learning how to be better disciplined and how to teach my children the value of hard work. Allow your children to discover what they want and have them work for it, don't just give them what they want."

5

Some Issues
For Consideration

|||||||||||||||||||||||||||||||||||||||||||||||||||||||||||||||||||||||||||||||||||||||

A s you take your journey through the world of music education, there are some issues that you will want or need to consider. In this chapter I will address the following issues and offer suggestions and possible solutions to some problems that may arise.

- Eligibility/Fit of the Program

- Recruitment of Homeschoolers Into the School Program

- Instrument Rental or Purchase

- Individual and Group Lessons

- Finding a Private Teacher

- Commitment to Systematic Learning

- Practicing

- Technology

- College Admissions

- Parents as Role Models

Eligibility/Fit of the Program

Many music programs have minimum age requirements or skills your children must have already accomplished before they will be able to participate. These skills can range from simply being able to follow directions to passing a minimum competency music skills test. Be sure to ask the music programs you are considering what they require.

A Suzuki program trainer told me that she advises trainees to accept very young children into their programs based on one very simple test: the child should be able to follow directions to do three unrelated things consecutively. For example, the child may be told, "(1) take this stuffed animal to the couch and set it down, (2) bring me your shoes that are by the front door, and (3) when you come back to me, turn around in circles until I tell you to stop." If the child successfully accomplishes these things without further prompting, then he is ready to begin formal music lessons. This tests the child's memory of the instructions, and ability and willingness to successfully respond to the instructions. Other programs for early music instruction simply have a minimum age requirement.

Participation in your local public school music programs may be a welcoming experience, or you may find it to be a difficult one. A few states do not allow homeschool students to participate in public school programs. Most, however, have created policies to accommodate homeschoolers, and some public school programs are actually recruiting homeschoolers' participation. Homeschoolers may find that participation in the local school's jazz program, string quartet program, mariachi ensemble, or madrigal choir may offer them experiences they can't find other places. Find out what the expectations are of the district, school, and teacher, and decide whether you can make the commitment that would be required for participation. Be prepared to play or sing an audition, and you can expect to provide your own transportation to and from the school. Most programs will require you to be in attendance for full participation in daily or multiple-weekly rehearsals, and at all scheduled performance events.

You may have opportunities to participate in district or state events as a homeschooler only if you pay a fee, or participate in related programs. For example, in Illinois if you are not enrolled in a public school program, it is necessary for each homeschool family to pay a "participating school" fee in order to participate in Illinois Music Educators Association activities such as auditioning for IMEA District and All-State bands, orchestras, and choirs. If you have been able to get permission from your public school to participate in their middle or high school music program and your child already is a member of that program, then the fee would be paid by the school.

Research the quality of the programs you are considering by asking the opinions of people who already participate. Find out about the programs' successes, and why people are continuing. Check the credentials of the programs. Are they members of a larger parent organization or do they stand alone as a single entity? What is the background of the teachers? What do they require for certification or licensure of their teachers? What awards have they won or honors have they earned? Check references that are given to you by the organization, as well as outside sources you may be able to find.

Beware of untrained or non-certified teachers and staff members. Some organizations are great marketers, but lack quality and substance. Quality music programs will be excited to tell you of the successes of their current and former students. If you call references and hear anything negative, filter that information based on the needs of your children. Are you required to pay fees up front, or do you pay as you go? Does the organization offer a makeup lesson if your child is ill and must miss? If they do, will you be charged for an additional lesson? In most studios, you are paying for the time they are setting aside for you, therefore whether you are there or not their fee must be paid. If teaching is their livelihood, they can't afford to have occasional or frequent empty slots in their schedules with no pay. Ask about possible "hidden" fees, such as requirements to purchase tickets to performances, exclusive instrument rental contracts, required uniform purchases, and music purchases. These costs may be necessary to run a quality program. Just be sure to gain a clear understanding of the policies and requirements before choosing your musical path.

Finally, interview the teacher just as you would interview a child care worker or nanny, keeping your child's personality in mind. Take your child with you to meet the teacher. There should be a chemistry between the student and the teacher that is readily apparent at the first meeting. Get the facts, and use your instincts to size up the program when choosing what the best fit will be for your child.

Recruitment of Homeschoolers Into the School Program

During times of financial difficulty in public schools, enrollments often drive the staffing and quality of the programs. It can be in the best interest of the public school music programs for teachers to identify homeschool students and find ways to involve them in their bands, choirs, orchestras, and other music course offerings. This will potentially increase their enrollments and enrich their ensembles. Homeschool students are often very dedicated, inquisitive, and hard working, and can bring a fresh perspective and new strength to a school program.

Recruitment of homeschoolers can take many forms. Find out who the homeschoolers are in your area by looking for homeschool organizations and family support groups. Hang out at the local YMCA or Park District during daytime hours on a school holiday, and you will find many homeschoolers participating in programs. Word of mouth also goes a long way in identifying students who may already be involved in music. Suzuki, Kindermusik, and Yamaha programs may be willing to offer you the name of families you could contact, and those families, in turn, may lead you to others.

Youth symphonies, community bands, and community choirs are good resources, and you can ask people in any organizations that you are affiliated with — your church, your synagogue, your neighborhood, your bowling league, your spouse's colleagues, and even other staff members at your school. School secretaries are the greatest resources I've ever found. Ask them for names of homeschoolers they know, or who they recommend to ask. Check with your current students and their parents to help you identify homeschoolers. Some of them may even have been homeschoolers in previous years. Your Music Boosters organization may be willing to create a list of homeschoolers for you, or they could advertise for families in a newsletter or on their website.

After identifying families of homeschoolers in your school district, you can begin contacting them to invite them to participate in your program. Use multiple means of communication. Send a letter to their homes, email them, and most importantly call and talk to the parents. Having a two-way conversation gives you the opportunity to answer any questions they may have, and gives you insight into their concerns. Explain what your program has to offer their children, and how your program might benefit by their participation. If you've had homeschoolers in your program before, describe the experiences they've had and the benefits they've gained from being involved. Be sure to emphasize experiences you can offer them that they may not be able to have elsewhere, such as performing in concerts at the school, participating in marching band, auditioning for district and all-state programs, traveling with the band, choir, or orchestra, and being involved in music with other students in their community. Also be ready to give anecdotal information about how your students have benefited by having you as a mentor. Don't be bashful about sharing stories about how you've touched the lives of your students. Homeschool parents want to give their children opportunities to develop relationships with people of good character who can guide them and help them grow into fine young adults. They will be gratified to hear about the impact you've made on other students' lives.

Finally, you can broadcast your interest in homeschoolers by putting an article in the school's newsletter, advertising in the local newspapers, and putting up posters in local places of business, with their permission. This will help the word to get out that you welcome homeschoolers, and once you get the ball rolling you may enroll more students than you ever anticipated. It might take more work initially to identify, communicate with, and nurture these students, but you ultimately have the ability to positively affect the lives of many more students than you have on your present school class rosters.

Instrument Rental or Purchase

I am often asked by parents, "which is best — to rent or to buy?" While on the surface there are obvious benefits to both, here are some things to consider.

Typically the quality of a rental instrument is lower than the quality of one you would purchase. Music companies don't like to put expensive instruments into the hands of students as rentals because they know the families will be returning the instrument to the store and they often don't care for the instrument as well as they would if they owned it. Without ownership, families have less monetary commitment to the instrument. However, many instrument rental companies can offer families a quality that is acceptable to the teacher, and the cost can be *greatly* reduced from a purchased instrument.

One benefit to renting is that many companies offer a "rent-to-own" plan in which a large percentage, or all, of the rental monies paid over time will apply to the purchase of the instrument. If you'd like to upgrade to a better quality instrument at the time the rental fees reach the value of the instrument, the companies often will offer to have you pay the difference to get the better instrument. Another benefit to renting is the ability to trade up from one size to another. Violins, violas, cellos, double basses, flutes, harps, and guitars all come in small "kid-sizes" for students who are smaller than full size, and many rental plans accommodate a trade to the larger sizes as children grow.

If you have more than one child and you'd like to own a smaller size instrument for the younger siblings to use after the older child has grown out of it, then perhaps you'd prefer to purchase the instrument. Some families purchase the smallest instrument to hang on the wall or save as a memento. The smallest violins, for example, come in 1/32nd size, and displaying the tiny instrument in the home can bring back many fond memories of their child in the early years of musical development. Still others purchase instruments so they can share them with their extended families and friends. An instrument co-op can save a significant amount of money for the families involved.

For older children who are beginners on a full-size instrument, a higher quality instrument will give them better success. Beware of the garage sale instrument and the "attic Strad" that may be a good price but could end up costing more in repairs than the instrument is worth. Grandpa's fiddle might have sentimental value, but it could be swarming with mites, have cracks in the wood, and need new strings, pegs, chinrest, shoulder rest, bridge, and horsehair for the bow. All instruments are designed to be played, and instruments that have been sitting for a long time will eventually deteriorate.

When you're ready to purchase an instrument, research your options and get the assistance of a teacher. Teachers are unbiased resources of expertise who know what a quality instrument is and, if the teacher knows your child, can make recommendations specific to your child's needs. I always ask my students to find three to five instruments from various music stores in our area, and then have them set an appointment with me to play the instruments. Without knowing prices, I number them and play each one to determine which sound and feel I like the best. Then I have the student play on the instruments while the parent and I listen. We can usually pick out a good instrument that will serve the student well over time. If none of these instruments are appropriate or of interest, continue to search other places. If you can't find an instrument you want, or you live in an area that doesn't have instruments available for purchase, instrument dealers across the country are willing to ship instruments on approval for you to try out. Don't give up until you find exactly what you're looking for.

Individual and Group Lessons

Some families mistakenly think that enrolling their children in a music class or taking them to private music lessons is all they need to do to ensure a high quality music education for them. It takes both, however, to become an accomplished musician. Children need a comprehensive musical experience of private and group instruction in order to develop a love for music and become successful at making music.

The Orff Schulwerk method of music instruction is based on what children do naturally: sing, chant, beat on things, and clap their hands. These activities take place in a social environment with others, beginning in the family with their mother, father, and siblings, and extending to other social settings. Orff classes, extended family gatherings, homeschool groups, church groups, and playgroups offer opportunities for children to exercise their knowledge of music. Individual lessons in voice, piano, or another instrument will come later, after the child has developed basic skills and learned to love singing and responding to music. The reading and writing of music will also come later.

The Suzuki method uses the "mother-tongue approach" of teaching very young children to listen and respond to music as they learn to play an instrument, just as in infancy they listen to their mother's voice and begin to form the sounds of their native language. Starting early, listening to musical recordings daily, repeating musical elements through practice, being encouraged with sincere praise, and learning from the parent who learns to play the instrument before the child are characteristics of the Suzuki method. Weekly lessons with a private teacher are scheduled, and the parent works together with the teacher to check for understanding and accuracy in the child's playing.

Accompanying these early musical experiences in the family and with the private teacher, are group lessons with other children of the same age or ability level. During the group lessons children perform for each other, participate together playing the songs they've learned, and encourage each other, promoting a spirit of cooperation as they make music together. Both private and group lessons together create the best scenario for the child's success in learning music.

For the child who is beginning musical training during the elementary, middle, or high school years, a balance of individual and group lessons is also highly important. In the case of the student who is always in a group setting without individual instruction, bad habits can begin to form in technique, posture, and tone. As skilled as a group teacher may be, there is no substitute for an expert working one-on-one with your child. In group lessons, time can be wasted for your child while another child's needs are being addressed, it is difficult for the teacher to hear each child's tone and give the detailed feedback the child may need, and important habits of technique or posture may easily be overlooked.

On the other hand, when a child receives only private lessons without group instruction, the joy of music making with others is missing. There often is a lackluster, mechanical approach to the playing or singing of a student who has only received private instruction, even when the student has been taught to perform musically. Inherent in music making is the need to share the experience with others, and to respond to others who are participating with you. Just watch children who come together for a group class or rehearsal, and see the joy in their faces and in their actions! I have often observed children be moved to tears when they leave a summer music camp or when they've performed their final concert of an

academic year. They will miss their friends, even if only tem-
porarily, and they will miss the joy they've experienced making music with others. These are *powerful* human experiences
that cannot be duplicated in the individual teacher/student
setting.

Finding a Private Teacher

One great benefit parents and students have in the field of
music, from the earliest instruction through college-level
musical training, that differs from most other fields is the
opportunity to choose your teacher. Always keep in mind that
the choice is a two-way street. When you're seeking a teacher
you'll want to gain as much information about the teacher
as possible, and the teacher wants to know something about
your child before agreeing to take her on as a student. Ask to
have a "sample" lesson. Many teachers are willing to do this,
often at no charge, so both parties can be sure the fit will be
right. Visit the studio and observe the teacher teaching other
students, with permission of course. Some programs require
a minimum number of observation hours before allowing
you to enroll. Find out as much as you can about the teacher's
background and qualifications, but also pay close attention
to the interaction between the teacher and the students you
are observing. Is it a serious setting? Is there humor in the
lesson? Does the teacher connect with the student the way
you'd like to see your child connect with the teacher? By the
end of the lesson, do the children and parents clearly understand what they need to do during their practice sessions
through the week? Is the lesson well organized? Do you sense
an underlying negativism? Do you sense a joy in the learning
process? You have the responsibility to select a teacher who

will make a good fit for your child, and you will need to be patient as you go through this selection process. Ultimately you will be glad you went to these efforts, for the rewards will be well worth your time and patience.

Homeschool families can pool their resources and hire a teacher just for their children if the economics and logistics can be worked out. I know of a young woman who graduated a few years ago with a master's degree in music, looking for a job in the difficult and competitive market of violin performance. She had begun teaching three children in the home of a homeschool family during the two years while she completed her degree. After she graduated, word had spread about her effective teaching and wonderful manner with the children. This family did not want to lose her as their teacher, so they found other families in the area who were interested in lessons, and they invited the teacher to "live" at their house three days a week, teaching their children and the children of the other homeschool families. The teacher traveled back to her hometown three hours away, and taught lessons there during the remainder of the week. This created a very comfortable living for her, and she was able to build her program in the home of the first family. As she gained more and more students, eventually she was able to afford an apartment in each town. She continued to travel between the two towns for several more years, nurturing and teaching the children. She had become such an integral part of the families that the children not only learned great musicianship, but they also loved her as if she was a regular member of their family. This situation worked beautifully because these families highly valued her as the teacher and mentor of their children, and they were willing to invite her into their home to live with them while she built her career. When you're looking for a teacher for your children always keep their best interest at heart, and don't ever underestimate the value of thinking outside the box of your own experience to create something that might not have been done before.

Commitment to Systematic Learning

Having taught music for 33 years, I have had many students enter my classroom with a desire to "get a little music." They listen to music and enjoy singing or playing with their friends, or they played an instrument for a year or two, quit lessons, and are coming back to get a little more. Music keeps tugging on their hearts. For these students, while getting "a little music" instruction is better than none at all, it is evident that they are not committed to nurturing their talents and abilities to a level of technical and expressive proficiency that will continue to satisfy their desires throughout life.

Becoming an accomplished musician requires steady, systematic progress and a commitment to long-term learning and practice of skills. Even the most innately talented people don't just sit down at a piano, for example, and start playing. Of course, we've all heard of exceptions to this, but the exceptions are rare. Almost all children have the ability to learn music, and given an adequate amount of high-quality instruction and consistent practice, children can become quite musically accomplished. Whether or not a child is talented does not determine his fate as a musician. Parents have often said to me, "I really don't know whether my son is talented because I have no ear for music, so if you think he's doing okay I guess we'll keep him involved," or "Music is a mystery that I will never understand but if my daughter continues to enjoy it, I'll keep encouraging her." The problem with these statements is that parents aren't making a commitment to encourage their children in the academic pursuit of the knowledge of music, whether they are talented or not, or whether they enjoy it or not. As with all learning, there are certain to be ups and downs, highs and lows throughout the process, and enjoyment comes with the accrual of knowledge and skill.

Parents would never say to their children, "As long as you demonstrate talent in mathematics we'll continue teaching you math," or "Because you're enjoying reading about history then we'll continue to encourage you and allow you to get history books from the library." The pressures created in our schools by the requirements of No Child Left Behind have unfortunately required school districts to question whether they can afford to put resources into a sound musical education for all children. But the powerful ability music has to touch the hearts, souls, and minds of children, the discipline it teaches them when they learn to practice in a step-by-step, systematic way, and the attraction children have for listening and for expressing themselves through music, all lead to music as an excellent choice for serious study.

Parents must make a commitment to the study of music on behalf of their children, just as they do with other subject areas. Children will have their highs and lows in the learning process, at times enjoying the musical activities and experiences, and at other times finding them to be difficult work. Nothing worthwhile comes without a price. But the hard work of systematic study and practice produces the ease of an accomplished performance or the joy of new knowledge. When a parent makes the commitment to support the child throughout the whole process, the musical success of the child is inevitable.

Practicing

Practicing is a necessary ingredient in the learning of any skill or ability. Parents should arrange for a space with adequate lighting and proper equipment (music stand, pencil, etc.), and provide a regular time for practicing so the child will get into the routine of doing it. Just as it is necessary for your children to brush their teeth or go to bed at a certain time, practicing is a necessary part of the process of learning. Children do homework to accomplish their goals in other subjects, and practicing is the homework for learning music. When practicing becomes a habit, the pain of hearing a wailing child not wanting to practice will be eliminated.

The quality of the practice time counts. Some teachers will be explicit about what is expected during the practice sessions by explaining what is to be practiced, what level of achievement is expected, and how many repetitions are required after that level is reached. Others may be less clear. Be certain to ask if you have any questions about what the child is expected to do, and also what you will be required to do during the child's practice time. Because this is a great commitment, the two parents can share responsibilities, attending lessons and practicing with the child alternately every other week, or one parent working with one child and the other parent working with another child. Older siblings can also take on some of the responsibility. These decisions will be important for you to make as you begin a formal program of music instruction. Whoever is in charge of the practice time will need to know what to look and listen for, and take responsibility for the child accomplishing the goal before moving on to something else.

The length of the practice time is also an issue to consider. I've experienced a whole gamut of possibilities both as a student and as a teacher — using a rigid practice chart with an expectation of a certain number of minutes each day or week; having a recommended amount of time, say, "twenty minutes a day, or until you get tired"; having an assignment with specific goals to accomplish and not stopping until they're accomplished; and having no guidance except to be told to practice a certain passage or technique. My best advice to parents is to set the expectations of what is to be accomplished on a daily basis, and once those goals are achieved, the practice session is over. After a few days or weeks using this as your guide, you will begin to know approximately how much time it will take for your children to accomplish their goals, making adjustments as needed. Very young children may not be able to do everything in one setting, so practicing twice a day for, say, ten minutes each can be a reasonable solution. If you have an advanced student, you eventually will be able to quantify a reasonable number of hours per week they will have to practice in order to accomplish the goals set by their teacher. One mistake to avoid is to "cram" practice — doing several hours of practicing over a couple of days instead of spreading it out over the course of the week. Consistent, daily progress will produce the best results. As your children grow and mature, help them make good decisions about how to balance their practice time with everything else in their lives.

Some programs celebrate students who practice every day for months and years at a time. Total days of practicing are applauded in concert venues, and the children reap the benefits of their labors through their ability to perform at a high level. Others teach children that an occasional break — on weekends, in the summer, or when they are ill — is a good thing in order to keep a balance in their lives. You will need to determine what works best for your family, always keeping in mind that *consistent* practice is the tool that sets up your child for success.

Technology

Children are sponges for technology. When given the opportunity, they will spend hours playing an electronic game or figuring out how to navigate their way through a website. In music, your children can be easily motivated to learn if you take advantage of the latest available software and hardware.

Using technology can be as simple as recording your child practicing on a video or audio recording device and playing it back for analysis, or it can be as complex as the most advanced technology allows. The Technology Institute for Music Educators (TI:ME) is available to assist musicians in applying technology to improve teaching and learning. Visit their website at <www.ti-me.org> to learn about the latest advancements and recommendations for the use of music technology. Using electronic keyboards and synthesizers, producing music through MIDI (musical instrument digital interface), using recording and sequencing devices, notating music through music software, using instructional/practicing software, creating web pages or electronic portfolios through multimedia software, and managing computer systems, labs, and networks related to music are just some of the areas in music technology that can enhance your child's education.

Parents who have an affinity for technology can be great role models for their children, learning software along with them and offering their knowledge and expertise in computers or electronics they may already have. With technology rapidly changing, parents and children can take advantage of the latest developments by staying abreast of these changes, updating their knowledge of available software and equipment, and reading journals on related topics.

Some publications on music technology that are available are *Electronic Musician Magazine, Study Outline and Workbook in the Fundamentals of Music* by S. Estrella, *The Art of Sequencing* by D. Muro, *Teaching Music With Technology* by T. Rudolph, and *Experiencing Music Technology,* 3rd *edition* by P. Webster & D. Williams.

More information on technology and software can be found in Chapter 6, "Additional Resources."

College Admissions

In order to be considered for a major or minor in music at a college or university, students must pass a rigorous audition on the instrument or voice in which they are applying. The requirements vary from school to school, and no special consideration, either positive or negative, is usually given for public, private, or homeschooled students.

In addition to the audition, most colleges require a normal application for admission, a separate music program application, a music theory test, and for some degree programs, an interview. Although research on the performance of homeschoolers in college music programs is limited, admissions officers are generally quite interested in homeschoolers as potential students. Homeschoolers often perform at a very high level both musically and academically, and they tend to be self-directed and visionary in their goals. Homeschoolers who participate in all-state ensembles, youth symphonies, choral unions, Bands of America competitions, or other recognized high-performing musical ensembles are often targeted by colleges and recruited heavily.

Students who are interested in continuing to play or sing in college but are not planning to pursue a major or minor in a music field are openly welcomed by most colleges. The universities in our state have begun focusing on these non-music majors by inviting them to audition for their bands, choirs, and orchestras, and occasionally offering them scholarships to participate in these ensembles. At a recent college concert I attended, the conductor proudly announced the various majors of all the students performing in that ensemble, particularly emphasizing the non-music majors. The concert not only was an impressive musical performance, but was a celebration of the myriad talents of the members of the ensemble.

For information on college admissions policies for homeschoolers in general, you can visit the website of the National Center for Home Education, a division of the Home School Legal Defense Association, <www.hslda.org/docs/nche/000002/00000241.asp>. There you will find a listing of homeschool admissions policies for many colleges and universities. You can call the admissions office of any college or university in which you are interested and ask for their home-school policy.

For directories of college and university music schools and faculty information, you can talk to a high school counselor in your area, research information at your local library, or look online at the following sources:

Bridge To Music

> <www.bridgetomusic.com>
> Bridge to Music is a resource guide for musicians of every level. The quickly expanding directory features over 3,000 music schools, classes, workshops, music festivals and a brand new private teacher listing. It includes a directory of over 1,400 college and university music schools.

Directory Of Music Faculties In Colleges And Universities, U.S. And Canada

<www.music.org/cgi-bin/showpage.pl?tmpl=/infoserv/facdir/
facdirinfo&h=63>
This directory, published by the College Music Society, identi-
fies over 37,000 music faculty members in the U.S. and Canada
and lists over 1,800 schools or departments of music in higher
education in the U.S. and Canada. The directory can be purchased for $175, or $75 for members (including shipping and
handling).

Music Schools Directory

<www.aboutmusicschools.com>
Music Schools is a worldwide directory of music schools. There is
also information about music instruments, careers in music, music
education, and all that you want to know about the music industry.

Strings Magazine

<www.stringsmagazine.com>
At the Strings Magazine website do a keyword search for colleges and universities that teach string instruments and you
will find a brief description of the school, tuition, room & board,
degrees offered, faculty, campus description, and contact information. Over 500 schools are listed.

Wikipedia List Of University And College Schools Of Music

<en.wikipedia.org/wiki/List_of_colleges_and_university_
schools_of_music>
This is a listing by country of schools of music, including links
to each school. There are 45 countries listed, as well as external
links to other directories.

Parents and Teachers as Role Models

Adult ensembles, music classes and summer music camps are increasing by leaps and bounds in our country. With the aging population in the US, people are finding they have time to pursue interests they've never had time to enjoy before. Brain researchers are encouraging older adults to find activities to change their patterns of thought and behavior in order to enhance their quality of life in later years. Adults who take part in musical activities that are new and different from those that are familiar to them experience a higher quality of life, less memory loss, and experience fewer instances of Alzheimer's and other diseases.[1] As a result, colleges, universities, music camp organizations, YMCA's, churches, and community organizations have begun to develop music courses and opportunities for adults both young and old.

Parents and teachers of homeschooled children can take advantage of this new wave of musical opportunities for adults. Children learn by example, and watching their parents pursuing a new musical frontier can be a powerful model for the child. Learn to sing, learn to read music, learn to play a musical instrument, take lessons to become more proficient on an instrument you already know, learn a musically related skill such as violin making, or join a performing ensemble. The adult establishes himself as a lifelong learner. He puts himself in a position of learning something new, a position all children know very well! Children are constantly learning new skills and experiencing the discomfort that goes along with the development of those skills. Adults who choose to learn a new musical skill can identify with their children's learning and empathize with their discomfort by experiencing the learning of a new talent first-hand, step by small step. The adult therefore becomes a role model, not only for the musical skills acquired, but also for being willing to put himself in the position of a learner. What better gift could you give your children than demonstrating for them how exciting it is to learn a new skill? The wonderful thing about music is that, once you've learned the skill, you can participate in it along with your children.

Following are some opportunities and information designed specifically for adult music instruction. You can check with the colleges and universities in your area for additional options.

Adult Music Student Forum

<www.amsfperform.org>
The Adult Music Student Forum, Inc. (AMSF) is a nonprofit corporation that promotes the educational and performance interests of active adult non-professional, non-collegiate instrumental and vocal students, whether they are beginners, persons returning to music after an extended absence, or advanced students, and whether study is formal or self-directed.

Chimneys Violin Makers Workshop, Tuscon, AZ

Contact: 614 Lerew Rd., Boiling Springs, PA 17007-9500. (717) 258-3203. <www.chimneysviolinshop.com> edwardcampbell@sprintmail.com
This is a violin making, repair, and restoration workshop for those who have an interest from beginner to professional. Making and restoring bows is also included in the curriculum. Week one is devoted to setup. Week two is devoted the making of new instruments. Weeks three and four are devoted to making and restoring instruments and bows, including rehairing bows.

Depaul University Adult Music Classes

<music.depaul.edu/cmd/Programs/Adult/Instruction.asp>
Programs in adult class piano, music theory, the art of song
interpretation, and several instrumental and vocal ensembles
are available through this Chicago-based university. All levels of
adult musicians are welcome.

The Hartt School Community Division Of Music And Dance

<hcd.hartford.edu/music/adult_program.htm>
Adult musicians of all interests and abilities can find instrumental
ensembles, chamber choir, private lessons, classes in piano and
voice, and workshops through this University of Hartford program.

Lark Camp — World Music & Dance Camp, Mendocino, CA

Contact: PO Box 1176, Mendocino, CA 95460. (707) 964-4826.
<www.larkcamp.com>
registration@larkcamp.com
Imagine idyllic days and nights in the magical redwood forest
filled with all the music, dance, and good times you could possibly stand. You are free to take as many or as few of the workshops offered for beginners and professionals. There are jam
sessions 24 hours a day and big dances every evening. This is
truly a unique total immersion into the joys of nature, music,
and dance. Violin and fiddle styles are include: original fiddle
tunes, Quebec and dance fiddle, hurdy gurdy, Gypsy jazz, old-
time Clare-style Irish fiddle, and more.

New Horizons International Music Association

<www.newhorizonsmusic.org/nhima.html>
New Horizons Music programs provide entry points to music
making for adults, including those with no musical experience

at all and also those who were active in school music programs but have been inactive for a long period. Many adults would like an opportunity to learn music in a group setting similar to that offered in schools, but the last entry point in most cases was elementary school. We know that for most of the last century, about 15-20 percent of high school students nationally participated in music. From that, we can estimate that at least 80 percent of the adult population needs beginning instruction in order to participate in making music. New Horizons Music programs serve that need. Bands, orchestras, and other ensembles are listed by state, and summer camp information is available.

Schoolhouse Fiddle Camp For Beginners, Avoca, NE

Contact: PO Box 671, 504 Garfield St., Avoca, NE 68307-0671. (402) 275-3221. <www.greenblattandseay.com> g-s@greenblattandseay.com
This camp includes some of the basics and fun of fiddling, such as performing in public, practice techniques, reading music, playing by ear, and jamming. Fiddling styles include: bluegrass, Cajun, Irish, Klezmer, old-time, and newly composed tunes by campers. Movement and singing is included in the instruction.

Scor! String Camp, Rochester, NY

Contact: 67 Pembroke St., #1, Rochester, NY 14620. (585) 313-4319. <www.stringcamp.com> info@stringcamp.com
Classes include adult instruction from beginners to advanced string players, and piano for advanced players. The camp includes private lessons, chamber ensembles, technique sessions, fiddling/cello ensembles, jam sessions, and more.

The Truth About Adult Music Training

<piano-lesson-software-review.toptenreviews.com/the-truth-about-adult-music-training.html>
This is an article written by Pamela S. Stevens in which she discusses the differences between children and adults learning music. She addresses self-direction, level of physical discomfort, insecurity or embarrassment, and prior experience and application.

Woodland Chamber Music Workshop For Adult Amateur Musicians

<www.woodlandchambermusic.org>
The Woodland Chamber Music Workshop is a place where adult amateur musicians of any instrument and all skill levels come together for a weekend of small-ensemble playing and coaching, seminars, chamber orchestra, and fun on the beautiful North Shore of Lake Superior in Northern Minnesota.

6

Additional Resources

|||||||||||||||||||||||||||||||||||||||||||||||||||||||||||||||||||||||||||||||||||||||

Publishers and Printed Music

Published materials in music can be found in abundance. Hal Leonard Corporation is the world's largest music print publisher that has been publishing and distributing publications for virtually every type of instrument and ensemble for over 60 years. Categories of publications on the Hal Leonard website, <www.halleonard.com>, include *Piano Songbooks, Choral and Classroom Music, Music for Guitar/Bass/Folk Instruments, Solo Instrumental Literature*, and many others. There are reference books about music careers, songwriting, music business, audio technology, and biographies about popular artists and classical performers. Information can be found about every instrument and vocal technique. Published church music, band and orchestra literature, and percussion play-alongs are also available.

Of particular interest to homeschool families may be music materials that are designed for self-teaching. The "Play Today" Instructional Series published by Hal Leonard is a method of instruction that can be used by students who want to teach themselves, or by teachers for private or group instruction.

The series offers a complete guide to the basics, designed to offer quality instruction, well-written songs, and a professional-quality CD with 99 full-demo tracks. Students can learn at a pace that suits them, as they open the door to the world of music. The series is written for most instruments and voice, including a vocal book and books for violin, bass, trumpet, trombone, flute, clarinet, alto saxophone, piano, guitar, recorder, drums, ukulele, and banjo. Books are available in levels one and two, each including tips and techniques, how to read standard notation, how to produce a quality sound, instrument fingering charts, and a glossary of musical terms. The CD provides instruction by the teacher, as well as accompaniment music to the songs in the book.

Other self-teaching materials are available as software (see next section on "Software and Music Technology").

If you are searching for printed music, publishers who are members of MPA (Music Publisher's Association of the United States) are listed on the MPA website at <mpa.org>. Following are a few of the larger publishing companies where you can find an abundance of printed music:

Alfred Publishing Company, Van Nuys, CA
Belwin-Mills Publishing Corp., Van Nuys, CA
Boosey & Hawkes, Inc., New York, NY
Breitkopf & Haertel, Wiesbaden, GERMANY
C. Alan Publications, Greensboro, NC
C.F. Peters Corporation, Glendale, NY
Carl Fischer, LLC, New York, NY
Concordia Publishing House, St. Louis, MO
Curnow Music Press, Inc., Nicholasville, KY
Disney Music Publishing, Burbank, CA
Edwin F. Kalmus & Company Inc., Boca Raton, FL

EMI Music Publishing, New York, NY
FJH Music Company, Inc., Fort Lauderdale, FL
G. Schirmer, Inc., New York, NY
G.I.A. Publications, Inc., Chicago, IL
Hal Leonard Corporation, Milwaukee, WI
Highland/Etling Publishing, Long Beach, CA
J.W. Pepper & Son, Inc., Paoli, PA
Kendor Music, Inc., Delevan, NY
Latham Music Ltd., Winston-Salem, NC
Luck's Music Library Inc., Madison Heights, MI
Macmillan/McGraw-Hill, New York, NY
Masters Music Publications, Inc., Boca Raton, FL
Mel Bay Publications, Inc., Pacific, MO
Mona Lisa Sound, Edgewater, NJ
Neil A. Kjos Music Company, San Diego, CA
Oxford University Press, New York, NY
Schott Music International/ European American Music,
　New York, NY
Shawnee Press, Inc., Nashville, TN
Silver-Burdett / Pearson, Lebanon, IN
Sony / ATV Music Publishing, Nashville, TN
Southern Music Company, San Antonio, TX
Summy Birchard, Inc., Miami, FL
Theodore Presser Company, King of Prussia, PA
Vanguard Music, Stockholm, NJ
Warner/Belwin, Van Nuys, CA
Wingert-Jones Publications, Paoli, PA

Software and Music Technology

Perhaps another area of interest may be in software and music
technology. You can purchase any of the leading music software,

cutting edge hardware for the special needs of the musician, tutorials and reference materials, DVD's, and sheet music from a variety of sources through the Hal Leonard website.

Included in the software available are several series' for self-teaching music instruction from a variety of publishers. A *Beginner's Piano/Keyboard Course* and *Beginner's Guitar Course,* published by eMedia, can each be purchased in four volumes. A CD-ROM instructs the student from the very beginning stages of learning the instrument. As the music plays, correct fingerings are shown to guide the student, and interactive multimedia lessons are designed throughout the series. A series published by Allegro Multimedia entitled *Piano Wizard,* is another piano keyboard course of instruction. Its "Premier" package includes the actual piano keyboard, along with the educational software.

A series of software programs for elementary and middle school students entitled *Groovy Music,* published by Sibelius, is available in three volumes. The first volume, *Groovy Shapes* for ages five to seven, teaches children the basics of sound, rhythm, and pitch, allowing them to create their own music in the "Create" section of the software. Volume 2, *Groovy Jungle,* is designed for seven to nine-year-olds. This level teaches children about more complex textures and instruments, allowing them to experiment more with their own compositions. In the third volume, *Groovy City,* children ages nine to eleven are introduced to question and answer phrases and the blues scale, giving them more tools to build into their more complex compositions.

A series of five software programs published by Sibelius are great tools for educating your budding young musicians. Students can use them independently, or with the help of a tutor, parent, or teacher. *Starclass* is a complete elementary music program software package with over 180 interactive music lessons. *Sibelius Instruments* is a multimedia encyclopedia of over fifty instruments with photographs, notated examples, high quality recordings, and quizzes to help students learn to recognize sounds. A comprehensive software package for ear training and aural tests, *Auralia Academic,* is specifically designed for classical, jazz and rock/pop students with special exercises on jazz and contemporary scales, chords, and progressions. The upgraded *Musition 3 for Windows* is music notation software including eight new topics, new administrative features, a bright new interface, and the ability to create custom levels in any topic. Finally, *Compass* is a software program designed to help students learn how to compose. The lessons lead into composition projects such as theme and variations, songwriting, sonata form, and blues. All of these programs are in CD-ROM format and are highly interactive.

Following is a list of software that is widely used by many performers and teachers, and can readily be found through academic or music publishing houses. This by no means is a complete listing.

Band In A Box — Band-in-a-Box by PG Music, Inc. is an intelligent automatic accompaniment program for your multimedia computer. Just type in the chords for any song, choose the style, and Band-in-a-Box generates a complete professional quality arrangement.

Finale® — This is a family of music notation software offering various levels of professional need for the composer, including Finale®, Finale® Allegro, Finale® PrintMusic, Finale® Songwriter, Finale® NotePad, and Finale® Reader, by Make Music, Inc.

GarageBand—Apple publishes this instructional software that teaches you to play piano and guitar (instruction for other instruments can be purchased additionally), allows you to plug a keyboard or electric guitar into the computer for access to over 100 other instruments, lets you jam with a full-screen band, and gives you the opportunity to record and mix your songs.

Logic Studio—This set of software includes everything you need to create, perform, and record music. Also published by Apple, it includes Logic Pro 8, MainStage, Soundtrack Pro 2, Studio Instruments, Studio Effects, and Studio Sound Library.

MiBAC Music Software, Inc. (Music Instruction By A Computer)—MiBAC is music software incorporating lessons in music fundamentals (level 1), chords & harmony (level 2), and jazz.

Practica Musica®—This is a complete tutor by Ars Nova Software for both music theory and ear training, including a beginner's course, an exploration of a theory textbook course, and an advanced level course in theory and ear training.

Sibelius—Sibelius is music notation software for educators, students, composers, arrangers, copyists and musicians of all kinds. It allows you to easily write, refine, hear, scan, and print beautiful scores.

SmartMusic®—This music learning and accompaniment software by Make Music, Inc. is a powerful tool for students and teachers. It allows teachers to send assignments to students, students to practice with a computer getting constant feedback on their playing or singing, and teachers to assess student performances.

Websites

If you do a search online for "homeschool music" you will find nearly 1,000 responses. Some websites are large companies that provide effective tools for learning, others are schools or directories that provide lessons, and still others are private programs or families that include information about their musical activities.

Here are some websites you might like to investigate for more information about music and homeschooling*:

<http://books.google.com/books>
   At this website do a search for "homeschool music" and you will find a book entitled "How to Organize (Just About) Everything" by Peter Walsh. In it is a section on how to homeschool your child, including nine steps you should take to organize the process. Music and sports are mentioned.

<http://harmonyartmom.blogspot.com>
   This homeschool mom tells how busy homeschool parents can incorporate music appreciation and fine arts into their lessons. Included are blogs, recordings, podcasts, suggested composers to study, and a section entitled "Why Have Art and Music In Your Homeschool? No More Excuses."

<http://home-school.lovetoknow.com/
Homeschool_Music_Lessons>
   This website includes information on why music is important and how parents can teach music at home even if they are not trained musicians.

---

*These websites are not necessarily recommended, but are listed only for your reference.

<http://homeschooling.gomilpitas.com/materials/Music.htm>
These are materials for a general music curriculum, musical instruments, lessons, and sheet music.

<http://www.homeschoolmusic.net>
This is a homeschool music association in the greater Lansing, Michigan area.

<http://landofmusic.com>
This is a music curriculum for classroom or homeschool use.

<http://lifestrums.com>
This organization will help you organize music groups and classes in or near Louisburg, Kansas.

<http://makemusic.com>
MakeMusic, Inc. is a world leader in software and systems for musicians. Their mission is to develop and market solutions that transform how music is composed, taught, learned, and performed. MakeMusic publishes Finale® music notation software and SmartMusic® accompaniment and learning software.

<http://nces.ed.gov/pubs2001/HomeSchool/support.asp>
This is a 1999 article from the U.S. Department of Education outlining support from public schools that may be available to homeschoolers.

<http://nces.ed.gov/pubsearch/pubsinfo.asp?pubid=2004115>
This report was published in 2003 from the U.S. Department of Education about how many U.S. households homeschool their children and the reasons why.

<http://nhme.org>
The National Homeschool Music Ensembles of Tecumseh and Ann Arbor, MI can be found at this website.

<http://thepianostudent.wordpress.com>
This is a free music resource directory, including printable sheet music, music theory worksheets, nursery rhyme sheet music, and links to composers, careers in music, and information about music history.

<http://topsytechie.wordpress.com/2008/08/08>
A homeschool mom gives her advice on available technology and music software for homeschoolers. There are seventeen titles listed with a short synopsis of each one.

<http://triviumacademy.blogspot.com/2007/01/classical
-music-study-plan.html>
This is a classical music study plan for kids. It lists systematic units and materials for reading and listening.

<http://www.angelfire.com/or/mtdewbydo/art.html>
At this website you will find free online music theory workbooks, free interactive piano lessons, printables, and much more.

<http://www.apple.com/logicstudio>
This is a set of software that includes everything you need to create, perform, and record music; Logic Pro 8, MainStage, Soundtrack Pro 2, Studio Instruments, Studio Effects, and Studio Sound Library.

<http://www.ars-nova.com>
Ars Nova Software, LLC, provides a trilogy of music education and composition software, including Practica Musica®, Counterpointer®, and Songworks™.

<http://www.childrensmusic.org>
This non-profit website offers musical resources for performers, teachers, parents, and kids.

<http://www.homeschooldiscount.com/hsp/music.htm>
You will find a curriculum for K-12 music instruction by
grade level at this website.

<http://www.homeschoolingonashoestring.com/music.html>
Listed at this website are free and low-cost music items,
instruments, and lessons.

<http://www.mhschool.com/music>
Macmillan/McGraw-Hill is a leading publisher of elementary educational materials from Pre-Kindergarten to Grade
8. The "Spotlight On Music" series includes textbooks for
PreK-8th Grade students and is available at this website.

<http://www.mibac.com>
MiBAC Music Software, Inc. (Music Instruction By A
Computer) is music software incorporating lessons in music
fundamentals, chords & harmony, and jazz.

<http://www.musicforhome.com/curriculum.html>
Pfeiffer House Music has prepared a Christian based music
curriculum for K-6 classroom or homeschool students.
Instructions, worksheets, flashcards, and audio CD accom-
pany the texts.

<http://www.musictogether.com>
This is an early childhood music program from birth to
Kindergarten.

<http://www.notation.com/SpecialInterest-Childrens
-Music-Ed.htm>
This website offers notation music writing software. It
provides links to children's music programs including
the Cincinnati Classical Public Radio, Dallas Symphony

Orchestra kids' website, New York Philharmonic KidZone, Free Music Games, Tips for Parents, etc.

<http://www.ohmimusic.com/Why%20Music%20Ed.htm>
This website describes the result of research on the benefits of music education, including, "Twelve Benefits of Music Education," "Music's Top Ten Benefits for Parents," and "Music Education Facts and Figures."

<http://www.pearsonschool.com>
Pearson is a world-renowned PreK-20 educational publishing company, and publisher of the Silver Burdett series of music textbooks used in many public schools music programs. The complete K-8 series is available at this website.

<http://www.sibelius.com>
Sibelius is a powerful music notation software for educators, students, composers, arrangers, copyists and musicians of all kinds.

<http://www.swapnstuff.com/cat.php?cat_id=Music>
This website is for swapping items at very little cost, including CD's, DVD's, books, and textbooks.

<http://www.thecenter4thearts.org/musik.php>
This Cincinnati area music center offers summer programs, family music celebrations, homeschool world music lessons, and classes featuring the MusikGarten® curriculum.

<http://www.thejubileeacademy.org/articles/art_and_music_homeschooling_printables.html>
There are free printables on the topics of art and music at this website.

<http://www.wyzant.com>
This is a tutoring website that profiles tutors across the US. You type in the category and subject (for example, "music oboe"), enter your zip code and radius for your search, and you will find profiles of people in your area who are experts in that field.

Conclusion

Your journey into the world of homeschooling and your commitment to teaching music to children will, I hope, be in some way aided by the information in this book. There are so many avenues you can take, and I wish for you the greatest success as you make choices for you and your children. At the outset I stated that parents of homeschoolers want the best education possible for their children and are willing to take responsibility to find creative ways to offer them meaningful and exciting learning experiences. Because of your commitment to music education, and your creativity in designing a program that meets the needs of your family, you will truly ensure that you and your children will experience the unparalleled joys of accomplished musicianship. My sincere best wishes as you embark on this journey!

Endnotes

||||||||||||||||||||||||||||||||||||||||||||||||||||||||||||||||||||||||||||||||||||||||||||||||

Preface

1. Milman, Gregory J. "Class Act: Home is Where the School Is." *Washington Post* 23 Mar. 2008: B01
2. Bielick, S., Chandler, K., and Broughman, S.P. "Homeschooling in the United States: 1999." *National Center for Education Statistics* 02 Oct. 2001: 033
3. Princiotta, D., Bielick, S., and Chapman, C. "1.1 Million Homeschooled Students in the United States in 2003." *National Center for Education Statistics* 02 Aug. 2004: 115
4. Bielick, S. "1.5 Million Homeschooled Students in the United States in 2007." *National Center for Education Statistics* 18 Mar. 2009: 020

Chapter 2

1. Accepted February 2007 by MENC's National Executive Board. Copyright © 2007 by MENC: The National Association for Music Education. Reprinted with permission. http://menc.org/about/view/menc-position-statements.
2. Ibid.
3. Ibid.

Chapter 3

1. Based on Merriam Webster's Collegiate Dictionary (10th ed., 2001), in which "homeschool" and its variants are spelled as one word.
2. Accepted February 2007 by MENC's National Executive Board. Copyright © 2007 by MENC: The National Association for Music Education. Reprinted with permission. http://menc.org/about/view/menc-position-statements.

Chapter 5

1. Clark, Al. "Of Mind and Music: ECU Aging Study Explores New Pathways." *The Daily Reflector*. 21 June 2009. *Cox Newspapers*. Greenville, NC.

About the Author
|||||||||||||||||||||||||||||||||||||||||||||||||||||||||||||||||||||||||||||||||||||||||

Joanne May is Visiting Professor of Music Education at Elmhurst College in Elmhurst, Illinois where she supervises student teachers, teaches music theory and is conductor of the Elmhurst Chamber Orchestra. She taught 33 years in the public schools in Illinois, teaching all levels of orchestra, general music, and band, and serving as Music Department Chair and Orchestra Director at Glenbard East High School in suburban Lombard. She is an active guest conductor and clinician for workshops and festivals throughout the country.

She has had a number of homeschoolers in her classes over the years, both in her public school programs and as a teacher in a Suzuki studio. As the parent of two children, she has interacted with homeschoolers at Suzuki camps, studio music programs, community orchestras, church orchestras and YMCA programs for many years.

May is recipient of the "Those Who Excel Award" for excellence in teaching, was named Outstanding School Orchestra Director of the Year by Illinois ASTA, and was named Chicagoland Outstanding Music Educator by Quinlan and Fabish Music Co. The Glenbard Township High School District honored her with the Distinguished Service Award, and the Illinois Music

Educator's Association named her a recipient of the Mary Hoff-
man Award for Teaching Excellence. She is compiling editor of
*The String Teacher's Cookbook: Creative Recipes for a Successful
Program*, published by Meredith Music Publications, distrib-
uted by Hal Leonard. She is a National Board Certified Teacher,
and is immediate Past-President of the Illinois American String
Teachers Association.

Joanne received B.S. and M.S. degrees in Music Education
from the University of Illinois at Urbana/Champaign, studying violin with Paul Rolland and Homer Schmidt. She has completed post-graduate coursework in Music Education, Suzuki
Teacher Training, and Educational Administration & Supervision. She can be contacted at Elmhurst College, Irion Hall, 190
Prospect Avenue, Elmhurst, Illinois 60126-3296. Phone: (630)
212-7954; Email: jmay7954@yahoo.com.

More Teaching Resources for Homeschoolers from Meredith Music

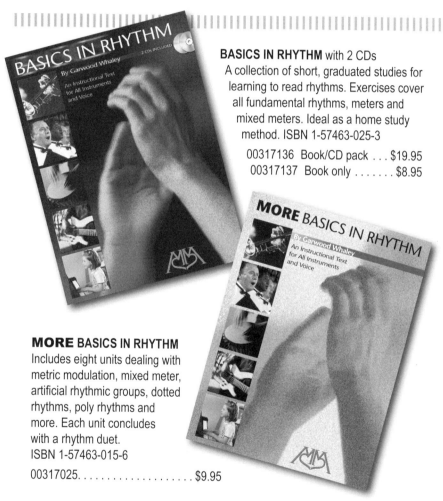